The Little Book on Digital Marketing

The Little Book on Digital Marketing

Keyword Research

JOSEPH STEVENSON

For my wife,

Kassie Stevenson

Thanks for putting up with the long hours
and unknown years of entrepreneurship. I
love and owe you everything.

Contents

01

Introduction

Why I Wrote This Book and How It Can Help

"Alice asked the Cheshire Cat, who was sitting in a tree, "What road do I take?"

The cat asked, "Where do you want to go?"

"I don't know," Alice answered.

"Then," said the cat, "it really doesn't matter, does it?"

— Lewis Carroll, Alice's Adventure in Wonderland

Why

The Purpose of This Book

I decided to write this book as the first in a series dedicated to digital marketing. I intend it to be a roadmap detailing where to go and in what order for maximum success. My hope is that it will provide a valuable resource to beginners and well-seasoned digital marketers who just need a good reference book.

I am often emailed and called for advice on digital marketing by competitors, students, potential clients, and others. Usually, I get calls because a website I was involved in marketing received higher visibility, creating a mad rush to find out what my secret sauce was for its success.

I don't believe in any secret ingredients, but instead I focus on doing the right things over a long period of time, which will inevitably lead to greater results.

This book and the books that will follow will focus on the different aspects of digital marketing that I've found will produce great long-term results. Each on its own should be a good resource, but together they will make a blueprint for your online success.

Things May Change Over Time

Since digital marketing changes constantly I would assume at some point this book would have outdated material. With that in mind, I will attempt to share general theory on how a specific skill or principle works, instead of specifically about a tool or website.

I will use websites as examples and case studies but my hope is to teach skills and not give a direct reference to a tool that may not be around in ten years.

As I wrote this book, Facebook and Pinterest were the top social media giants. If I had written this book 10 years ago that wouldn't have been the case. Back then if you had said Myspace would be dethroned everyone would have mocked you.

I am not going to speculate on which direction things will go, but the basic principles of finding your market, targeting it correctly, and getting in front of the right customers will be true regardless of what online niche will be controlling the traffic at any given time.

You May Disagree with Me

Digital marketing is a broad topic and interpreted so differently by a variety of experts. There are so many techniques that it would be impossible for me to write a guide and have it accepted by everyone.

With that in mind feel free to disagree with me. I would love feedback and you can participate in online chapter discussions through my blog at https://josephstevenson.com. Go to the university area and click on the blog/chapter you are currently studying. Under the comments, I would welcome feedback, corrections, or additions you feel are necessary.

Even if we disagree I will gladly publish your opinion as long as it is a professional response free from spam or vulgarity. You may also email littlebook@josephstevenson.com and I will publish your comments from there as well.

How

The Process

This book is dedicated solely to keyword research. It is the first in a ten-part series on digital marketing.

I will be publishing each book in this series in the order that I feel they should be read. By the end of the ten part series, you will have the main principles I use in my marketing firm to achieve consistent results for my clients and myself over time.

Chapter Structure

Each chapter is divided into six parts encompassing:
- How
- Why
- Case Study
- Goals and Actions
- End of Chapter Challenge, and

- Citations.

How: Once I have "sold" you on the idea my goal is to teach you how to apply it to your own situation. I will give you examples of how I have used the technique and other resources so you can do the same.

Why: This section will cover why this topic is important and how it can benefit you. It will contain examples and stories of success using this specific principle. Think of it as my sales pitch on whatever the chapter is on.

Case Study: This section will contain a real-life example of a company or companies that have applied the principle with great results.

Things to Ponder: In this section, I put the most relevant points to focus on. I suggest you re-read this book occasionally to brush up on the skills you've learned and the Things to Ponder section will give you the best overview and thought points.

End of Chapter Challenge: I believe we learn best by practicing, so each chapter will end with a challenge. Even if you feel like you know everything about a specific subject, do the challenge. It will help you retain what you learned.

Citations: I've listed all cited resources from the chapter here in case you prefer to wait until the end to look up the sources. I will also post the citations for each chapter on the blog for easier navigation.

One Final Note

I intend this book to help business owners, marketing managers, students, and really anyone interested in digital marketing.

There are so many online resources meant to give you eighty or ninety percent of the truth with the rest available for purchase in a subscription or package.

It can be frustrating when you're trying to learn a new skill to have some of the information withheld for a price. I hope that I can convey the full one hundred percent of a principle so you won't feel ripped off or like you'll need more information at the end of a chapter.

Although each chapter is set up to be read through in the order it was written, feel free to skip around and write in the margins. After all, this is your book as much as it is mine. Diving in will be the best way for you to learn a new skill. Let's get going!

02

Theory

"If the facts don't fit the theory.
Change the facts."

— Albert Einstein

Why

From Hunting to Fishing

I was raised in a small town about two hours from Las Vegas called Golden Valley, Arizona. We were close to the city of Kingman [1], which is where we went to church; I got my first job, and where I started my first business.

I was always inclined toward art as a child

and my parents encouraged me to practice my talent until I was good enough to enter competitions and fairs.

When I was sixteen I wanted to try my hand at being an entrepreneur, so I started asking local businesses if I could paint holiday scenes on their windows for about $30.00 each.

I can still remember the thrill of getting my first client. There is something about having a business owner say, "Yes, I will pay you for this service or product you've made," that creates a drive like nothing else can.

Quickly after starting my window painting business, I realized that nobody wanted to clean the paintings off the windows after the holiday was over. Many of the business owners asked me to come back and clean the paint off as well.

As time went on I realized I could make more money by cleaning the windows every month than what I'd make by painting them only once or twice a year.

After only a few months my decoration business turned into a full window cleaning company servicing homes and businesses all around the Kingman area.

I had officially gotten the entrepreneur bug and I really liked it.

Marketing as a Kid

I was seventeen while this was all happening and I didn't have much experience in running a business or doing marketing. I knew I wanted to work for myself and I had the drive to work hard -- but that was about it.

The Internet was still just getting started and there was no such thing as digital marketing at the time. I got all of my clients through referrals from friends or by directly driving to their office and knocking on the door. I didn't realize it at the time but the best thing I had going for me was my age.

Putting myself in my client's shoes, if I had a seventeen-year-old knock on my door and tell me he or she had started a business cleaning windows I would hire them on the spot.

Even if I didn't need my windows cleaned it would be hard to not support a kid who was trying to do something most teenagers wouldn't consider.

My business grew rapidly and soon I was servicing Bullhead City and Lake Havasu City along with my Kingman route. I had built a solid business by going around and hunting for new clients.

Getting to the Point

I'm giving you this backstory for a purpose. I spent the first five years building a business by knocking on doors for new clients. I had never considered there could be a better and much easier way to do things.

When you hunt you have to go out quietly, sneak up on your prey and attack before they have a chance to run away. Usually, the hunted don't want to be, and if you catch them the kill or sale comes with a struggle.

On the other hand, when you go fishing, it's a more relaxed process. You put bait in the water and wait. You can read, nap, or get a tan while your bait does all the work.

When I realized this principle it shifted my ideas about marketing by a hundred and eighty degrees. The rise of the Internet and search engines allowed businesses to stop hunting and start fishing.

If you had told me back then that there was a place in town where everyone was looking for a window cleaner I would have paid whatever I could to get in front of them.

How nice it would have been to be able to present my service to people who were actually looking for it instead of those who weren't.

Keyword research is the first in a set of tools that can help you begin fishing for customers. When you know what people are looking for and where they're searching for it, a whole world of possibilities opens up.

Tim Ferris in The Four Hour Work Week [2]

describes testing your niche by doing keyword research before you ever start your business. Using AdWords [3], Tim tested multiple titles for his book and saved himself from selecting a bad one by using keyword research to put his ideas in front of people who were already interested in what he had to say.

Similarly, you can use keyword research to test your business idea before investing thousands in dead or undesirable products or services. If you want to be an entrepreneur, you have to be willing to throw out ideas that don't work until you find one that does.

How

The Process of Keyword Research

You have to begin with an idea. Don't worry about whether it's a good idea; that's what keyword research is for. Instead just pick an idea that interests you and run with it. Don't worry yet about making money or how big the idea will be, we are only testing to see if there is interest in the concept.

Once you have the idea you can begin to determine its popularity and the level of interest it will generate.

For example, my idea will be guitars. My father played the guitar most of his life and he taught me to play when I was a teenager. I know enough about it to be able to make good decisions about the type of people that play guitar. Having this kind of knowledge up front isn't a requirement for success, but it does help if you have experience with the idea you want to promote. Otherwise, you will need to educate yourself first before moving ahead.

Now I can't just say "OK guitars" and have keyword research do the rest. Instead, I need to have a slightly more specific idea in mind. If you don't have one feel free to use mine until you get the hang of this process.

I'm going to focus my idea a little more by targeting wholesale guitar strings. Honing further, I am going to target musicians who are looking for a good deal on guitar strings. This should be a specific enough goal to get my research started.

Had I been marketing as a teenager I would have started knocking on random doors looking for guitar players that wanted to buy my guitar strings. Eventually, after knocking on hundreds of doors, I would find a few people that would purchase from me, even if only out of pity (people in Kingman are pretty nice).

There is a much better way to find buyers -- by using keyword research. I needed to know what keywords my buyers were using to find their product and then position myself to show up when they searched.

Think of keywords not just as online words typed into search engines but the actual interests of your future buyers. If you know what their interests are you will be able to position yourself to give them what they want.

Choosing the Pond

So I know I want to sell wholesale guitar strings, but I also want to get in front of people who are looking to buy guitar strings, not just everyone whether they play an instrument or not.

Let's pretend for a minute that the Internet doesn't exist but I still want to use the principle of keyword research to get in front of buyers. I don't want to hunt them down and convince them that they need what I'm selling. Instead, I want them to swim around like a fish, and then bite down on the bait. But instead of a bad outcome, they would just enjoy the treat.

The first thing we need to do is find out where our potential customers are. Ryan Pinkham in his article "Five Ways to See How New Customers Are Finding Your Business" [4] says that when you know how people are discovering your company, it gives you a chance to focus your marketing efforts so you can bring more customers through the door.

Taking the guitar strings example, ask yourself where those customers already are? When I look at it that way, the answer becomes so obvious I couldn't believe I wasted so much time doing cold prospecting. Musicians hang out in music stores, school band rooms, clubs where musicians play or watch other musicians play, hippie parks and the list goes on and on.

Getting in front of your customers isn't about convincing or selling but instead being in the right place at the right time, also known as fishing. Five hours of sitting in a music store selling my guitar strings would easily beat the same amount of time spent walking door to door hoping to randomly find guitar players.

The difference is that in one scenario the customer comes to me looking and in the other I am hunting them down.

The How of this Chapter

This chapter is about theory and is meant to get your mind in the right state for keyword research. The remaining chapters will focus on specific keyword types and how to find them.

If you don't quite understand the theory yet, re-read and apply as many scenarios as you can think of to the principle of fishing versus hunting. How to do keyword research can be answered with one question: Where are my customers?

When you know where the customers are that are looking for what you're selling, you'll understand the better way to do marketing. You will get more customers in a shorter time with this method and the principle of keyword or interest-based marketing will finally make sense.

Don't hunt your customers down, fill the watering hole and wait for them to come to you.

Case Study

Structure Rentals

Structure Rentals is a client of mine who offers large structures for rent to organizations needing space for a short time. They also cater to organizations needing temporary large spaces.

Due to the size of each job, and amount of equipment involved in a typical rental, the cost can rise easily into six-figures.

Since their target audience is extremely specific, we had to find keywords that would target decision makers making purchase decisions, but not get caught up in smaller industry keywords that were similar.

For instance, we couldn't target "tent rental" because we would get everything from camping to party tent searches.

We also couldn't target too specifically with a keyword like "20,000 SQ foot tent structure rental" because the search volume (which we'll go into in the next chapter) was way too low.

We decided to take the approach of finding where our decision makers were and position ourselves in front of them.

Using AdWords and other CPC platforms we were able to enter our audience demographics:

-Purchasers
-Convention Centers

-Casinos

-Event Organizers

Once we had the demographics set up for targeting we blanketed basic keywords with targeted ads. So if a purchaser from a high-level organization searched for tent rental our ad would show up with text identifying large portable buildings for rent to companies like theirs.

The result? We went from having about one sale per month to four. This may not sound like a lot but in an industry where each sale is worth a six-figure profit a quadruple result in sales is a major game changer.

What Can We Learn

Knowing our audience was the key to success. We were able to look at past purchasers to find out what they had in common, including job titles, authority, buying habits, etc. Once we identified who they were we placed ourselves in front of them; just like the idea of selling guitar strings in music stores instead of door to door.

The results speak volumes. We learned a valuable lesson in targeting, placement, and keyword strategy that would serve our business well over the life of our company.

Things to Ponder

1. What business idea do you have that can be tied to a keyword? For example:
Business idea: Tennis training
Keywords: Milwaukee tennis trainers

2. Where do your purchasers spend their time? What are their interests?

3. What are the search habits of your purchasers? What type of keywords would they look for to find what you are selling?

4. What are your purchasers buying? If they aren't buying tennis lessons what are they buying that's related?

5. Are you willing to change your business model to fit what they're searching for? Is what they are searching for "evergreen" or a trend that will be gone in a short time?

End of Chapter Challenge

This end of chapter challenge will require you to act out what you've learned so far. First, write down your business or business idea. No worries if you don't have one, just go online and type in "easy business ideas." This is just a challenge not a commitment to a new business.

Business Idea _____

Next, identify three places where potential customers spend their time. If you go with the tennis lesson idea you could write down the gym, tennis club, or an online tennis blog.

Place 1 _____

Place 2 _____

Place 3 _____

Write down what activity is happening at each location the majority of the time. The gym would probably be working out; the tennis club would probably be playing tennis, etc.

Place 1 Activity _____

Place 2 Activity _____

Place 3 Activity _____

Now identify what keywords would work with each activity. If place number one is the gym where people are working out, then the keywords might be "local tennis gyms," or, "tennis gym," and so on. Any keywords that are related to that activity or place will work. Again, we're trying to target people in the places they will be -- or will be searching for.

Don't worry about whether anyone searches for the keywords you write down. In the next chapter, we will use volume tools to check the validity of the keywords. The important thing is to have a list that focuses on fishing for new clients and sales, not the hunting method.

Citations

[1] Kingman Arizona
https://en.wikipedia.org/wiki/Kingman,_Ariz
ona

[2] Tim Ferris, Four Hour Work Week

[3] Adwords http://google.com/adwords

[4] Ryan Pinkham
https://blogs.constantcontact.com/how-
customers-find-business/

Online Resources

Online resources for this chapter can be
found at:

https://josephstevenson.com/little-book-
keyword-research-ch2/

Links to citations, discussions and submission of
additional resources by readers are available for
each chapter.

To be notified of future books in the Little Book on Digital Marketing Series please email littlebook@josephstevenson.com or visit our website at http://josephstevenson.com/little-book/ and enter your email in the form provided.

03

Volume

"Most startups actually start down and only go up if they catch the winds of market demand."

— Ryan Lilly

Why

Verify the Need First

In college I learned about supply and demand in my business classes. There is a graph that shows the prices people are willing to pay for a product and a graph that shows product supply.

The spot where they intersect is the

equilibrium point, which is where product pricing should be placed. If your price is too high, you won't capture as many sales.

If your price is too low, you will end up pricing yourself right out of the market.

To find the equilibrium point, you have to understand product supply and demand; otherwise you won't be able to calculate the price point.

In a similar fashion, you shouldn't choose focus keywords unless you understand the demand for those keywords along with the supply.

To put it plainly, you shouldn't target a keyword with excessive competition or supply. Additionally, you shouldn't target a keyword that doesn't have enough demand (or searches) per month.

By shooting for keywords that satisfy both supply and demand in a favorable way, you will ensure success for your business.

High Volume = High Competition

High volume keywords tend to have very high competition. I did a search through Ahrefs Keyword Explorer [1] for "Bluetooth speakers". The average monthly search volume for that keyword is currently over 100,000. It definitely hits our criteria for volume but the competition is so high that we would have to invest a significant amount to show up organically in search engines or Amazon.

Using the Adwords Keyword Planner [2] we find that the suggested bid is about a dollar per click. This wouldn't be too bad if it was a direct sale keyword or one that would drive a guaranteed customer. Unfortunately, it's so broad that we are going to pick up researchers, students, grandparents, and anyone else who wants to know what a Bluetooth speaker is, not just the buyers.

Finding a high volume keyword can be exciting at first but there are very few high volume keywords without high competition. Most businesses with large marketing budgets have already been targeting high volume keywords for years, which have driven advertising prices up for popular niches. This makes it increasingly difficult for smaller businesses to compete for popular keywords and use them to capture market share.

Low Volume = Low Interest

Low volume keywords present a different problem. Usually if you find a keyword with low competition, the volume is also so low that there wouldn't be a point in going after it.

Ahrefs Keyword Explorer shows that the keyword "monitor speakers with Bluetooth" gets less than 10 searches per month. This keyword has no competition, but there wouldn't be much of a point in targeting it either, since nobody searches for it.

Unfortunately, a lot of marketing companies use low volume competition keywords to impress their less knowledgeable clients. Using keyword tools, they will target those with extremely low competition, which gives them quick rankings. Erick Schonfeld, in a

Techcrunch article calls these "vanity metrics" [3]. While these may look good at first, they're really a flash in the pan, in terms of SEO. By "flash" I mean all flash and no substance.

Schonfeld tells us:

> It is important for startups to properly instrument the data they track so that they can get a handle on the true health of their business. If they track only the vanity metrics, they can get a false sense of success.

Some marketing companies count on these metrics to impress their unknowing and trusting clients who might realize too late that their "success" has been only skin deep with little or no measurable long-term results.

Finding Middle Ground

The key to successful measuring and keyword selection is through finding middle ground between competition and volume. We always want higher volume but not so high that it is unattainable.

Going back to our Bluetooth keyword

category, we found that the keyword "top rated Bluetooth speakers" has about 1,700 searches per month with a cost per click of about .60 cents.

1,700 searches aren't a large amount, but it's much better than 10 or less. Additionally, the cost per click average is low enough that you could do a successful Adwords [2] campaign to measure keyword validity for organic and paid marketing purposes.

How

Finding Volume for Keywords

The first step in selecting a good set of keywords is to find the volume for a general topic. I prefer Ahref's Keyword Explorer [1], but there are others that I use cross-check volume.

I will explain the process using the Ahrefs tool and then list a few others I have used without giving full explanations on each.

I have personally used all of these tools, and plan to continue to use them in my day to day keyword selection and studies. If you have additional tools that you think would be helpful, please feel free to comment on the blog related to this chapter, or send an email to littlebook@josephstevenson.com.

Finding Volume for Keywords

Using Ahrefs, go to the Keyword Explorer tab. The page should say something along the lines of:

Keywords Explorer

Get thousands of relevant keyword ideas with accurate search volume, keyword difficulty score and advanced metrics like Clicks, Return rate and Parent topic.

From here you can enter in keywords separated by commas. If you are using it for the first time, I recommend entering just one keyword.

For research purposes, enter "Bluetooth speaker."

What will come up is data related to that specific keyword, along with ideas and search suggestions.

I will cover keyword difficulty in later chapters, so lets just focus on volume for now.

It is very important to start with a broad keyword with no more than three words in the search. The reason is because longer keyword phrases turn out lower volume suggestions, leaving little room for middle ground keywords. By starting with high volume/high competition keywords you give yourself a lot of room to work down a list.

Click on the "View full report" button below the keyword ideas list. This will bring up keywords related to your initial keyword search. It should sort by volume automatically from highest to lowest. If it doesn't, click on the "Volume" tab, which is the third one from the left. That will run your sort.

The CPC tab is next to the volume tab. It tells us what the average keyword cost per click is. In this example, the keyword generated 61,544 suggestions, which is plenty to sift through for some possible targets.

Based on what our goals are we can decide what an acceptable amount of competition per keyword is.

For instance, about 15 spots from the top is the keyword phrase "ilive Bluetooth speaker." There are 3,800 searches per month for that phrase and the CPC is .50 cents. If we have a webpage selling these speakers, and our profit per unit is $50.00, the math helps us decide whether we should target this keyword or not.

The lower the competition the better our odds of making decent profit on a product or service. That is just general common sense in business.

Moving down the list, we can see other keywords with even more potential. The keyword phrase "Sylvania Bluetooth speaker" gets 1,600 monthly searches, which is about half of the previous keyword but the CPC is only .20 cents. This one might be a better option if we're looking for a high-conversion keyword for the cost.

I think one of the best keyword phrases based on first impressions was "outdoor Bluetooth speaker." This phrase brings in 700 searches per month, which isn't a lot, but the CPC registered at .0 cents per click. This means that the competition is so low; Adwords can't give an estimate on cost since there aren't many bids for it.

The goal shouldn't be to build a brand based on only specific keywords or products that currently have very low competition. Instead, start with a broad topic and narrow down to products or services that have less competition and are attainable. As your business grows you will be able to target more competitive keywords and capture some market from your larger competitors.

With the Bluetooth model, I would suggest being a Bluetooth speaker company that sells multiple brands. Then focus on the brands with less competition so you can drive traffic to them for a lower cost.

Other Tools

Ahrefs is my tool of choice, but there are others I like to cross-reference the data to before making any investments in time or money for a keyword phrase.

Keyword Revealer [4] is one of my favorite tools right now because it generates more keyword ideas than many other tools. It also gives helpful data on number of sites competing for the same keywords, and how good their SEO is to naturally drive traffic. It has an estimated profit on each keyword as well, which can be helpful for affiliate marketers.

Adwords Keyword Planner [2] I may get

some flack for this one since this seems a little obvious, but there is still value in using the Adwords keyword planner. Lately the volume is a little messed up, showing only very large ranges for each keyword. You will notice that a lot of the keywords will show 1 – 1,000 searches per month, which is basically unhelpful. I still use Adwords for CPC verification to make sure we could pay for clicks without breaking our budget.

SE Ranking [5] is one of the best tools I've found for organic keyword tracking. Used mainly for keyword ranking reports, they tend to have the most accurate keywords. Their search tool gives data on keyword popularity, which I then cross-reference to Ahrefs data.

SEM Rush [6] has tools focusing on SEO agencies. We use them for client reporting and I have found that the amount of data they store on individual keywords is pretty staggering. They are also adding more related keywords, which are nice, but so far they don't seem to pull as much data as Ahrefs. I would suggest using them as another backup tool for researching

keywords you have already selected that
need verifying on volume and competition.

Aim High Expect Low

One of my golden rules in running a business
is to aim high and expect low. I go after
keywords with a volume I would expect to
give me great results, and then I expect a
third of the success that should come from it.

I am rarely disappointed by the results of a
specific group of keywords by following this
method.

If you expect to find, target, and profit from a
set of keywords the first time, you will
probably end up disappointed. Keyword
research is a marathon, not a sprint, and
reminding yourself of that constantly is
helpful for morale.

Remember that you are not the only one out
there looking to find high volume keywords
with low competition, so trying again and
again is imperative for long-term success.
When you fail, and trust me you will fail a
time or two, reassess your strategy and try

again. Once you find your groove stick with it and the rest of the puzzle will come together.

Case Study

Final Grade Calculator

I was looking around on Flippa [7] for established websites for sale, and found Conquer College [8], a grade calculator website. The sellers of the site touted a healthy monthly profit from Adsense ads and seemed to not put much effort into driving traffic.

With a little research, I found that the main keyword they were focusing on was "final grade calculator" and its variations. The average search per month for that specific keyword was well over six figures.

The CPC was extremely low and the keyword difficulty (we haven't covered this concept yet) was under 20.

As a test, I decided to do my own trial and wrote a 2,000-word blog about final grade calculators. My personal blog has a healthy domain authority, and based on the data, I expected some quick indexing from Google and a little traffic.

What Happened?

Like any SEO centered marketing, the first few weeks were pretty slow. It took about a week for my blog to get indexed in Google which I found by typing in "site:http://josephstevenson.com/final-grade-calculator/" to Google to see the indexed page.

We didn't have any rankings until three weeks in, when we showed up on the second page. Not bad for a six-figure keyword! Since the competition was low, I decided to get a few natural links from some sites referencing my topic.

The next couple of weeks we jumped up to spot five on Google and higher on Yahoo and Bing.

Our traffic to the blog increased significantly, proving the keyword volume was definitely paying off even without a number one ranking.

What we Can Learn from This

After this test, I took the page down since my area of expertise is SEO and marketing, not education and calculators. I was getting a lot of head scratching from students finding the page and wondering why the rest of the site was about a totally different topic.

This test did prove to me that proper selection of a keyword with high volume and low competition can increase site traffic, sales, and reach very quickly and affordably.

Things to Ponder

1. What keyword topics are most related to your business or idea?

2. Do the keywords related to your idea have high or low volume? Does the volume support a high or low demand for what you offer?

3. Are the keywords related to your business

moderately or very competitive? If highly competitive, how will you compete for the traffic – through sheer capital, or creative promotion?

4. Do the high volume keywords related to your idea produce a targeted audience or are they broad and undefined?

End of Chapter Challenge

This end of chapter challenge will focus on learning to find high volume keywords.

First write down your general idea below. Make sure it is the broad idea, not the specific one, so if you are into restoring cars put car restoration or just cars.

Idea _____

Next using the Ahrefs keyword explorer [1] enter your idea into the search console. Click on the View Full Report button below the "Having Same Terms" section of the report.

___

Below, write three keywords that have at least 1,000 searches per month but less than 5,000 for this exercise's purpose. You should be able to do a trial account for free on Ahrefs.

Keyword 1 _____

Keyword 2 _____

Keyword 3 _____

Write the keyword below that has the lowest CPC in the range you selected. This will be the keyword to focus on in our next chapter on difficulty. Write down the keyword difficulty below as well which one is under the KD column.

Final Keyword _____

Keyword Difficulty _____

Citations

[1] Ahrefs Keyword Explorer
https://ahrefs.com/keywords-explorer

[2] Adwords Keyword Planner
https://adwords.google.com/ko/KeywordPlanner/

[3] Vanity Metrics
https://techcrunch.com/2011/07/30/vanity-metrics/

[4] Keyword Revealer keywordrevealer.com

[5] SE Ranking
https://seranking.com/keyword-suggestion-tool.html

[6] SEM Rush https://www.semrush.com/

[7] Flippa https://flippa.com/

[8] Conquer College
https://flippa.com/7726892-conquercollege-com

Online Resources

Online resources for this chapter can be found at:

https://josephstevenson.com/little-book-keyword-research-ch3/

Links to citations, discussions and submission of additional resources by readers are available for each chapter.

To be notified of future books in the Little Book on Digital Marketing Series please email littlebook@josephstevenson.com or visit our website at http://josephstevenson.com/little-book/ and enter your email in the form provided.

04

Difficulty

*"Difficulties strengthen the mind,
as labor does the body."*

— Seneca

Why

Defining the Difficulty

Keyword Difficulty, or KD, [1] is an extremely important part of keyword research that's overlooked most of the time. It is tempting to focus only on the volume of a keyword instead of its attainability.

Oftentimes we get so caught up in the luster of a high volume keyword, that we totally ignore the competition for it. This can be bad news for companies with grand dreams to gather clients with high difficulty keywords that are outside their budgets or abilities.

When doing keyword research it's just as important to define keyword difficulty, as it is to determine keyword volume. Volume is important because it signifies a demand for the keyword. Difficulty is also important to understanding the competition or supply of content or media for that keyword.

Let's Get Moving

I won't spend a lot of time defining keyword difficulty. It's a natural process that isn't set up by any corporation or organization. Instead, keyword difficulty is defined by search supply and demand.

If a new widget comes into the market with little press or mentions, the keyword difficulty will be low. As that widget gets popular it will become more expensive to advertise on websites.

Keyword difficulty works the same way; the

higher the searches, the harder it will be to rank or get in front of those people.

It's an organic occurrence; so don't get angry at the search engines or anyone else. I like to think of it as search capitalism at work.

Now let's chat about how keyword difficulty is determined and some techniques to help you compete for keywords with high difficulty.

How

The KD Calculation

There is a lot of speculation on how keyword difficulty is calculated. A lot of sites have differing opinions on the subject. However, they all agree on one thing: KD does actually exist.

Mike Goracke gives a pretty good explanation of how KD is calculated with his answer in the MOZ Community [2]. Mike says that the calculation comes down to three main points:

Competition. The number of pages indexed by a search engine for a query.

Authority. The ranking strength of a webpage as determined by incoming links to the page and the website (Domain Authority). Authority is based on both quantity and quality.

Relevance. How well ranking webpages match specific search queries. This includes on-page ranking factors like keyword presence and off-page signals like anchor text.

I agree with Mike based on my own experiences and will elaborate on his key points.

Competition

Mike talks about the number of pages indexed by a search engine, but I would expand that to the number of pages, media, videos, social shares, etc., for a query.

The Internet continues to evolve and stored information continues to be shared in different ways. Mike gave this answer in 2013, which is still pretty relevant in 2017.

However, there are more tools for accessing information now than there were in 2013.

The important point, is that competition for the keyword starts with the number of pages or media online that are fighting over it.

We already learned about how it's harder to rank a keyword with higher volume.] That's due to the number of pages being indexed for that specific keyword, with the more volume, the more competition. The more competition the higher the KD, and the more resources it will take to rank for that keyword.

Authority

Page authority is determined by a lot of different things, including the age of the site, links to the page, amount of content, social signals, page speed, and more.

Think of authority as quality. The better your page is set up the more authority you have. The longer your page has existed the more authority it has. The more online sites talking about your page – you guessed it -- the more authority you have.

Major search engines and traffic drivers will use page authority to determine whether to show your content in their results.

The real reason I and so many other SEO companies are in business is because new websites want to compete with sites that have been around longer with much higher authority. We're paid to get their names out in a healthy way, so their authority increases and they can rank in specific keyword niches.

To see a broad overview on page authority you can check out John Ramptons post at Forbes [3]. MOZ [4] has a good overview of page authority as well.

I will be covering more on page authority in the On Page Optimization volume in the Little Book on Digital Marketing.

Relevance

The next chapter is on keyword relevance so I won't spend a lot of time talking about it. The main point to understand is that relevance is a page score based on how well it targets a specific keyword query.

The biggest, and I mean the absolute biggest issue I find with SEO is that people are targeting keywords on pages that are completely irrelevant.

Clients come to me complaining that they want to rank for "Keyword A." When I analyze their page it is completely focused around "Keyword B". Often the differences between page relevance and the target keyword is as stark as penguins and polar bears.

What I always explain is that the search engine crawlers are not human. If they crawl an image they see the file name, the alt and title tags, and the compression of the image. If they crawl the text on a page they see what the text says, not what we hope to insinuate in the text. If we want to rank for "Widget A", we had better talk about Widget A.

How to Analyze and Overcome

Understanding keyword difficulty helps us to make good decisions on what keywords to target. It also helps us know how much we should focus on the authority and relevance of our own page based on competitor's websites.

In the previous chapter we looked into Bluetooth speakers and found specific keywords that had low CPC but high enough volume to be worth targeting.

The specific keyword we ended up choosing was "outdoor Bluetooth speaker." Using Ahrefs Keyword Explorer [5] we found the keyword difficulty for this specific phrase was 12. Ahrefs measures keyword difficulty mostly by page authority or number of backlinks pointing to the page. With a KD of 12, the analysis is that to rank in the top 10 on Google you will need backlinks from 13 individual websites.

I will cover backlinks later, but basically you'll need 13 websites to talk about your site with the terms "outdoor Bluetooth speakers." Once those 13 sites are crawled by Google or other search engines your authority will increase along with your rankings.

A KD of 12 is not bad and falls under the threshold of 20 that I like to work within. There are probably related keywords that have a more enticing KD with high enough volume to justify going after it.

Under the Keyword Ideas section there is the phrase, "big blue party indoor-outdoor Bluetooth speaker," that gets 500 monthly searches. The KD is set to 0, which means you need less than 10 websites to talk about you for your rankings to show up on the first page.

Getting a very low KD and high volume keyword is ideal as long as the keyword phrase converts for your business.

This keyword seems to fit pretty well and with a little more research could probably produce similar results as our previous keyword with less investment.

Tools

Although I use Ahrefs [5], there are a lot of tools to calculate keyword difficulty. Most take into account page relevance and the number of backlinks or authority sites needed to push your rankings higher in search engines.

For rankings on sites like Amazon, the weight is more in favor of page relevance than authority. Ecommerce rankings change if product sales and reviews are high. This changes the game a little, so first it's important to know where you want the traffic increases to come from.

Below are some of my favorite tools for measuring keyword difficulty. I have not put them in order of my favorites; so don't take that into consideration as you conduct your own testing.

Adwords Keyword Planner [6] With Adwords, I still prefer to see the average CPC for a keyword. It won't tell you KD but a higher CPC usually means a higher KD. Notice that a lot of the keywords will say 1 – 1k searches versus the more accurate volume listed on Ahrefs or MOZ.

SE Ranking [7] I use this tool regularly to gauge the relevancy of sites targeting the keywords I am researching. SE Ranking will crawl competitor landing pages to tell me how relevant their pages are for the keyword. It saves a lot of time when looking through Ahrefs at keywords that have low KD.

MOZ Keyword Explorer [8] The MOZ Keyword Explorer does it all by combining the difficulty score with a volume score for each keyword. Additionally, they have an opportunity score to help you decide how easy or hard it will be to target that keyword. I would recommend this for beginners who may be a little intimidated by data from some of the other tools

The Greater the Pain, the Greater the Reward

We tend to remember the hardest experiences in life with fondness. The long hike where we had blisters all over our feet, the difficult pregnancies, the long bouts of sickness, or unemployment, all teach us things we appreciate later in life.

The easier experiences are nice memories,

but they rarely teach or mold us like hardships do.

When selecting keywords, use the tools and your own intuition and experience to guide you. Don't be afraid to target keywords that have high volume and high difficulty since attaining them will be a much more satisfying experience than keywords that take no work.

I would recommend targeting keywords in the beginning that are easier so you can practice, but don't get hung up on staying in the shallow end of the pool forever. High difficulty keywords are, as their name implies, difficult, but the rewards pay off much larger in the long run.

Case Study

Raptor Websites

When I started SEO consulting it was out of my house in North Las Vegas. My company was called Raptor Websites and all of my clients came from referrals. I didn't even have a solid website at the time to send people to.

My business was built like I think every business should start; with friends and colleagues asking me to do things for money. It seems simple, but the realty is simple: If there isn't enough demand for your product or service, you probably shouldn't be offering it.

As time went on I began to get this question from potential new clients, "Why can't I find you when I search for Las Vegas SEO?"

The truth was that I hadn't put any time into keyword ranking for my business. I had enough leads that I didn't really need more work at the time, and so the idea of ranking for the sake of getting new clients wasn't really important.

At the time, I did think it would have been a nice selling point to be able to say "Google Las Vegas SEO" only to find me at the top of the search. At the time I thought I knew a lot about SEO, but the longer I do this, the more I realize there is so much to learn. On top of that, SEO changes almost constantly, so if quickly.

At that time, I didn't know about keyword difficulty, but I assumed it would be pretty hard to rank for an SEO keyword. My strategy was to build pages centered on that keyword phrase and then build authority the only way I knew how; by manually contacting other sites.

It took about a year of contacting other websites every day and writing for them, giving them advice, free work, whatever it took for them to write something about my business and link to my site.

There isn't a lot of glamour to this story. No tricks or gimmicks like we expect in our world of upselling programs and classes. It honestly was just one solid year of hard work and then consistent work afterwards.

I think I got lucky with my keyword. It does produce leads, which wasn't the initial goal. I didn't do research on how many searches the keyword was getting each month or how difficult it would be to even show in the top ten. I just thought "Hey that will give me some authority," and went for it. It could have very well been a keyword that produced no leads or results, and I might be doing something else now for a living, writing SEO off as something that never worked for me.

I am hoping this and the other books in the series will give you the ability to know if a specific keyword or goal will pay off -- before you put a year of your life into it.

The moral of this case study is that hard work will trump knowledge and experience. Again there was no trick or technique. I literally spent one week writing the content and then 51 subsequent weeks hustling and contacting anyone who would talk to me and build my authority.

These days I have better ways of doing it, but the lessons I learned back then were.

Things to Ponder

1. What keywords are most targeted at your business/organization?

2. What is the keyword difficulty of these selections?

3. How long will it take to build enough relevance and authority to your site to show up on the first page of your target medium i.e. Google, Amazon, etc.?

4. What resources do you have that will help you build relevancy and authority, i.e. copywriters, email lists, social media followers, etc.?

5. Is the keyword difficulty too small to make a dent in your goals, too large to be attainable before the trend is over, or in the middle?

End of Chapter Challenge

This end of chapter challenge will piggyback the last chapter challenge. Enter the final keyword you selected based on volume from the last chapter:

Keyword _____

Next using the Ahrefs Keyword Explorer [1] again, check the KD for the keyword you choose and enter it below:

Keyword Difficulty _____

If the KD is over 20, look through keyword suggestions and pick 3 other keywords to target based on the relevance of your site to the keyword (we'll talk more about in the next chapter), the volume of the keyword, and the difficulty (preferably under 20 to start). List the three keywords below that meet your criteria. These will be the target keywords to start with.

If your keyword is less than 20, look for related keywords that are also under 20, so you can have multiple keywords to target in upcoming chapters.

Keyword 1 _____ KD _____

Keyword 2 _____ KD _____

Keyword 3 _____ KD _____

Citations

[1] Ahrefs, Keyword Difficulty Tool,
https://ahrefs.com/blog/keyword-difficulty/

[2] Mike Goracke, MOZ, How Keyword
Difficulty is Calculated
https://moz.com/community/q/how-is-
keyword-difficulty-calculated

[3] John Rampton, Forbes, How to Increase
Page Authority
https://www.forbes.com/sites/johnrampton/
2016/10/24/how-to-increase-page-
authority/#68f48e143477

[4] MOZ, What is Page Authority,
https://moz.com/learn/seo/page-authority

[5] Ahrefs Keyword Explorer,
https://ahrefs.com/keywords-explorer/

[6] Adwords, Keyword Planner,
http://adwords.google.com/

Online Resources

Online resources for this chapter can be found at:

https://josephstevenson.com/little-book-keyword-research-ch4/

Links to citations, discussions and submission of additional resources by readers are available for each chapter.

To be notified of future books in the Little Book on Digital Marketing Series please email littlebook@josephstevenson.com or visit our website at http://josephstevenson.com/little-book/ and enter your email in the form provided.

05

Relevance

"Excellent!" I cried.

"Elementary," said he. "It is one of those instances where the reasoner can produce an effect which seems remarkable to his neighbor, because the latter has missed the one little point which is the basis of the deduction."

- Dr. Watson in **Sherlock Holmes** by Arthur Conan Doyle

Why

Let's Get Relevant

Keyword relevance is the simplest principle that I will discuss in this book. It's probably the most logical "Ah, that makes sense!" concept for people to understand.

Keyword Relevance measures the significance of a keyword to the media the keyword is pointing to. This could be an ad that shows up for a keyword and the landing page it points to, a video's content connected to a keyword in YouTube, or a local search in Google Maps based on the IP address of the searcher.

Information sites like Google make money by displaying ads or services for a price. Users will pay if they have already received a free service that they perceive to be of value. Sometimes the price isn't monetary, but paid in terms of putting up with ads or other requirements that are profitable to the site.

If you think about it, the most trafficked sites on the web are completely free.

The money they make is from advertisers who they allow to access to their users.

To keep their service or product profitable, advertisers must remain better than their competition.

With that thought in mind it makes relevance one of the simplest but most important principles in keyword research and marketing.

Don't be Evil

Most people don't know that Google has a motto. First introduced in 2000, "Don't Be Evil," [1] was Google's corporate code of conduct, but what does that mean?

The idea behind the motto was to put users first. At the time, a lot of Google competitors were selling off their user's information to the highest bidder. Much like Facebook [2], Google didn't set their sites on income first, but instead user experience.

Knowing their users would continue to come back if the best results were served from their platform, Google focused on the user first and worried about making money later.

The most profitable companies tend to take this route of user experience first and monetization second.

With this in mind, keyword relevance to the content being promoted is essential to success. Search engines will penalize keywords that aren't relevant to their websites. In the social and ecommerce world, it is almost impossible for a product or message to show up if it has irrelevant keywords.

If you Create it, they Will Come

Knowing how to find high volume keywords with a manageable difficulty score will give you a big lead over competitors. Knowing what the keyword want to target is half the battle. Knowing how to target it is the other half.

Focusing on creating relevant content using keywords with high volume and low KD will allow you long-term success.

There is always a way to sell to users what you have to offer. What you can't do is convince someone they want to buy something that is irrelevant to what they are searching for.

The point of this chapter is to teach you that the content/product/media that you create must be relevant to your targeted keywords. Otherwise you will end up with users coming to your page looking for something other than what you are offering.

As I mentioned in the previous chapter, it is one of the main issues I find when consulting on website SEO. Over 90% of the time, websites are targeting business owner names, brands, broad keywords, etc., without targeting keywords that actually drive customer sales.

Many times I've worked with client's whose websites only show up for unrelated content, like the business owner's name, because that's what they've been writing about.

If you want users that are looking for "plumbing in Sacramento," your content had better be about plumbing in Sacramento.

How

It's Simpler than you Think

Creating relevant content or media is actually simpler than most people expect. You don't need a lot of experience to successfully create content targeting specific keywords. You do however need to make sure you follow a few simple steps to ensure success.

After you have selected keywords with high volume and low KD, the media you create needs to pass a few tests to make sure it is properly optimized.

I have listed the most important criteria below:

Overall Site Relevance. The site hosting the media needs to be generally relevant. If you are looking to rank for "bed bugs" it is okay if the site is about pest control. If the site is about pine trees you don't have a very relevant site.

Page Relevance. [3] The individual page you highlight should specifically target the keywords you want users to search for. If the page is about "bed bugs," make sure it talks about bed bugs and nothing else. Page relevance is actually more important than site relevance even though they both help.

Keyword Density. The keyword you're targeting should be featured within the content at a rate of about 2.5%, according to Yoast [4]. Google prefers nice, readable text. Your text should be well structured and attractively written. Texts with a high keyword density do not read nicely. They are, in fact, terrible to read! Instead of using your focus keyword over and over, you should use synonyms if possible. Google actually recognizes synonyms to keywords now. With that ability, optimizing for a single focus keyword becomes silly.

So where does the 2.5% come from if Google is looking for rich content, not exact keywords? Well, the Yoast plugin will set off alarms if you use the targeted keyword in your posts more than 2.5%. This tool helps you focus on the topic surrounding your keyword with the keyword sprinkled naturally throughout.

Pulling them Together

To summarize the process, you need to target keywords that are related to the product or service featured on your website. Each keyword should have its own page that focuses specifically on that topic. Within that page you should target the keyword but not so much that it looks unnatural.

By following this process, you should easily overcome any content relevancy issues.

There are also many online tools that allow you to check your keyword relevance to the digital media you're trying to promote. I have listed some of my favorites below:

Tools

Yoast [5] is an on-page optimization plugin popular in Wordpress for website SEO grading. It is very helpful when it comes to keyword relevance for your on-site media.

It doesn't have the ability yet to crawl media other than text and images, but hopefully it will be able to check rich media like videos and other content soon for keyword relevance.

Adwords [6] I cite Adwords a lot but it's because they are still a very necessary keyword research tool.

Adwords gives a better rate to websites with higher relevance to the ads being displayed. This is calculated based on quality scores [7]. The idea is that ads representing the page they are directing users to will have a much higher satisfaction rate than ads that send users to a non-relevant page.

In turn Google rewards these ads by driving down the CPC so they can show more often with better rankings than competitors with higher CPCs, but less relevant pages. I find Adwords to be a great resource for checking page relevance for specific keywords.

Wordstream [8] is an SEO software company with tools for grading websites. The relevance-scoring portion of their report shows the keywords used along with the relevance to the overall content. This is extremely helpful to gauge if you are diversifying but also staying relevant.

When Starting, Keep it Simple

Since we have discussed how important keyword relevance is and how to focus on it properly, it's time to relax.

People can smell a fraud from a mile away. Nobody wants to be sold something, instead they want to experience content and partake in what they're interested in.

Whatever your product, service or information, stay true to what you want to present and worry about the keywords, volume, and difficulty later.

If you go the other route by focusing only on what easily drives traffic, you might be successful, but your content will be so relevancy-centric that nobody will be interested in actually doing more with it.

Case Study

Event Rentals

I began working with an event rental company a few years ago because of their struggle to target the right keywords and make relevant content.

They are the leading provider of LED dance floors for parties, conventions, and any event that is looking for an interactive floor that changes with pressure and sound.

They also rent out everything from DJ booths, to couches for conventions here in Las Vegas. They have provided equipment and props to everyone from Cisco to Amazon and are a leader in their industry.

I was brought on to work with them because their website, which had a lot of age and authority, was failing to rank well in search engines for the keywords they were targeting.

Past firms and employees were unable to correct the rankings, so when I showed up there was a lot of head scratching on what to do next.

After some research I found that the biggest issue was relevance of page content for keyword targeting.

Although they have one of the largest selections of arcade games for rent, the page listing the games was focused on images named with numbers.

When search engines crawled their page for indexing, the only content readable was a mix of random numbers and letters generated by their camera. Not the best way to make relevant content.

After some analysis we made major changes to the site's content. Our work wasn't technical or difficult; we just made changes to the text and the naming of the images.

For the arcade page, we added content that explained each game within the context of it being for rent. With a geographical target of Las Vegas, the location became relevant naturally.

Within three weeks the target keywords began moving up the rankings of search engines simply because the content on the page matched the keyword they were targeting.

We didn't build any backlinks, do press releases, social ads, or PPC; we just made the content more relevant.

As of today, they are the top-ranking provider of party equipment rentals, live cover bands, arcade rentals, interactive LED dance floors, and more. They also cover the entire U.S., providing dance floors and more to conventions and events from L.A. to Miami.

Things to Ponder

1. What keywords are most targeted at your business/organization?

2. Of these keywords what media targets them? Webpages? Videos? Images?

3. When looking through the media what is the main topic? When others look at the media what do they take away from the topic?

4. How natural is your media? Is it full of sales language or the complete opposite? What is the purpose of the media? What about it is engaging and relevant to what you are targeting?

End of Chapter Challenge

This end of chapter challenge is meant to stretch you outside any myopic tendencies you're having towards your own content and media. It is natural to assume we are doing things right, but usually a nice dose of constructive criticism can go a long way.

Without doing any edits, pick something from your business or organization that you've been trying to promote. This could be a YouTube video, a website, pictures, a social media profile, etc.

Write below what the content is; i.e. Facebook Page, Website, etc.

Content _____

Now without looking at the content or media, write down the intended topic that you wanted to market or target.

Topic _____

Now write down your intended audience. This could be anyone, and if you hadn't picked an audience, do it now. If you are an educator, then students are your audience. Be as detailed as possible. Don't just put students but 3rd grade students.

Audience _____

Choose a trusted friend, preferably someone with the skills to evaluate your content or media. Ask them to answer the same questions. Have them be as detailed as possible. The idea is to find out what they think the content or media is about and whom it is intended for. Do this with three different people to get their opinion. Use this as practice to determine how well you're targeting keywords and how relevant your keywords in relation to the media and content. Don't explain to them what you are doing since the key is to get a fresh perspective on your content.

Friend #1's Analysis

Topic _____

Audience _____

Friend #2's Analysis

Topic _____

Audience _____

Friend #3's Analysis

Topic _____

Audience _____

Citations

[1] Wikipedia, Don't Be Evil
https://en.wikipedia.org/wiki/Don%27t_be_e
vil

[2]Wikipedia, History of Facebook
https://en.wikipedia.org/wiki/History_of_Fac
ebook

[3] Adwords, Relevance: Definition
https://support.google.com/adwords/answer/
14089?hl=en

[4] Yoast, Keyword density in a post-panda
world https://yoast.com/keyword-density-
post-panda

[5] Yoast, http://yoast.com

[6] Adwords, http://adwords.google.com

[7] Adwords, Check your Quality Score,
https://support.google.com/adwords/answer/
2454010?co=ADWORDS.IsAWNCustomer%3
Dfalse&hl=en

[8] Wordstream, Keyword Relevancy and Popularity Ranking
https://www.wordstream.com/keyword-relevancy

Online Resources

Online resources for this chapter can be found at:

https://josephstevenson.com/little-book-keyword-research-ch5/

Links to citations, discussions and submission of additional resources by readers are available for each chapter.

To be notified of future books in the Little Book on Digital Marketing Series please email littlebook@josephstevenson.com or visit our website at http://josephstevenson.com/little-book/ and enter your email in the form provided.

06

Short Tail

"Victory is reserved for those who are willing to pay its price."

- Sun Tzu

Why

The Attractiveness of Short Tail

Short tail keywords are broad phrases people use when searching [1]. Examples of a short tail keyword would be any phrase that is two words or less. So a short tail keyword could be: Eggs, scrambled eggs, egg whites, chicken eggs, etc.

Marketers love these keywords because they drive a lot of traffic, usually ten times more than long tail keywords, which we'll cover in the next chapter.

Based on data from Raven Tools [1], short tail keywords get about 20% of the total search volume online. This means, while there aren't a lot of keywords that make up short tail keywords, but the ones that do drive traffic by millions per month to larger websites.

It's important to understand how short tail keywords work so that when you're researching keywords for your organization, you know the pros and cons of targeting them. Speaking of the pros and cons, let's list a few.

Pros of Short Tail

Volume. Short tail keywords make up the majority of online search volume. Individual short tail keywords commonly get millions of searches per month, which rake in huge profits for the companies that control their traffic.

Authority. Short tail keywords provide a huge amount of authority for site rankings. If you Google "Egg," incredibleegg.org [2] is the first result. Besides the commercials with the clever jingle, being the number one site on Google gives authority to this organization over their competitors.

Higher Bids. If you are a monetized website with high traffic for short tail keywords, you will generally get more ad money per impression than if you're relying on long tail keywords. There are so many large companies willing to spend enormous amounts on marketing, and these higher bids allow them to control more of the market. This in turn means higher profits for the controllers of short tail keyword.

More of Everything. Generally, the company who controls the traffic gets the lion's share. More newsletter sign-ups, more social media followers, more traffic, and more sales. Websites that control short tail keywords tend to be the most profitable in their markets.

But every action brings an opposite reaction. There are always cons to everything, especially in the keyword research game. I will list just a few below.

Cons of Short Tail

Competition. Short tail keywords are the most competitive in the world. On average, the cost to rank these over long tail keywords can be 100 times greater. Larger companies are driving the competition for these big-volume keywords.

This makes it very difficult to compete if you have a small ad budget.

Cost. Unless you have an almost unlimited budget, short tail keywords can be difficult to advertise for a long period of time. Some keywords can cost upwards of $100 per click due to the competition.

Broadness. As mentioned in seopressor.com [3], conversions on short tail keywords are much lower because they're so broad. Someone searching for eggs could be looking to buy eggs, cook eggs, hatch eggs, or do a report on eggs for school. The brand recognition is great, but straight conversions are often fairly low.

Attainability. With the high competition and high cost of these keywords, it is often very difficult to improve their visibility. This can be extremely frustrating and costly. Going after competitive markets is the name of the game for some businesses, but unfortunately most of the time Goliath beats David.

With Understanding Comes Respect

Understanding the complexity of a situation before entering it will help you succeed. This is certainly true for short tail keywords.

Once you understand the difficulty of capturing any share of the market with a short tail keyword, it becomes more real -- and often, intimidating.

The purpose of this chapter is not to make you afraid of short tail keywords. Instead, I plan to take the opposite approach, and actually go into how you can capture market share with competitive short tail keywords.

However, you do need to understand the difficulty inherit with short tail keywords if you are going to be successful. If you expect it to be easy, you will most likely write-off short tail keywords as impossible.

Properly measure the difficulty and competition, and then target for success. Short tail keywords will take longer than any other keyword to master, but the rewards can be extremely high if done correctly. Let's jump into the "how" of short tail keyword rankings.

How

Time and Money

I never said it would be easy, I'm only saying it's worth it.

Nikhil Ganotra in his article about ranking for short tail keywords [4], explains his tactics for ranking. He uses long tail keywords (which we will discuss in the next chapter) to capture market share on short-tail keywords.

The idea is that targeting and ranking for less competitive long tail keywords, will help you eventually gain ranking for short tail keywords by default in the same category.

This is definitely good strategy, but again, something we will discuss later in the next chapter.

Instead, I want to focus on how to rank for short tail keywords and directly capture some of the search volume from these monsters. As the sub-title implies, it will take both time and money.

Time

The majority of websites or media that capture short tail keyword traffic have been around a long time. Luckily for us, a long time in the world of the Internet isn't really that long.

Today we think that a 25-year old website is ancient, I guess technically, that is quite a while in Internet time. The reality is though, that it really isn't that long in the span of a life or business timeline.

When I was a teenager, the Internet was just getting started. AOL was the main search engine and dial-up was the only way to connect.

Back then, it was normal to yell at your sister for picking up the phone and interrupting your Internet connection. In the past 10 years the online landscape had changed so dramatically that it wouldn't even be recognizable to anyone who stopped using the Internet 10 years ago.

Time is such a commodity because it's a non-renewable resource. Every day that passes is gone forever, and what we do each day can't be changed or undone. This has created a sense of urgency and frantic workaholic behavior for many of us trying to get ahead as quickly as possible.

If you don't have 25 years to age a website so it ranks well for short tail keywords, there are other options. This is where money comes in to play.

The important thing to remember is that an aged site usually trumps a new site. Aged sites have more recognition, backlinks from authority domains, press, and general buzz than any new site. This gives them a massive head start in the short tail keyword game.

Let's talk about how money can fix the time issue and increase visibility for your brand.

Money

With enough money, you can get your business further ahead in terms of effort and time.

Flippa.com [5] is an online marketplace for domains, apps, and established websites. By searching for established domains, you can find 20+ year old websites with a history of short tail keyword ranking and revenue. The price usually is in the hundreds of thousands for these sites, but for those with enough money, it allows them to skip to the head of the line, saving valuable time.

Usually the high priced sites are from individuals who have made their profit and are looking to retire or exit to another business.

Other sites, like Godaddy Auctions [6], allow you to purchase domain names that have been around awhile or are extremely valuable due to their short tail keyword rankings.

Going to the website, you will see in the "buy now" section hundreds of domains for sale in the seven-digit range. These are domains with no website or traffic. The potential on these domains is so high that they are sold regularly for high dollar amounts without any history except the domain.

Using Both Together

I recommend leveraging both time and money for success with short tail keywords. By purchasing an aged domain, you overcome the time that a domain needs to rank for short tail keywords.

Additionally, you can purchase press, ads, and recognition online from most major outlets. Many start-up organizations raise hundreds of millions just for advertising their product. Although they think that money will guarantee success, often it's just enough to allow the new company to enter the market and capture some share of the search.

To rank for a keyword that is short tail without time or money on your side is almost impossible. I am not a dream-killer, but I believe in taking calculated risks. Targeting a Super Bowl-sized ad audience with a postcard budget isn't a smart move.

Do your research and determine the volume, competitiveness, and nature of the keyword. If you don't have the budget to compete for short tail keywords, move on to long tail. Once your business is established you can always move back to short tail.

Understanding what it takes will allow you to make better decisions instead of blindly targeting keywords without a specific success plan.

Case Study

Male Enhancement

An unnamed company that produces a male enhancement product for lasting longer in bed contacted me recently.

I received a call from their marketing team after they had hired an SEO consultant who had demolished their search engine rankings.

They had time on their side with a well-aged domain, but the consultant had completely ruined their rankings by deleting established pages and creating new non-targeted pages with no redirects from the old pages.

Their rankings dropped for many keywords including the short tail keywords that were driving the majority of their traffic.

The good news is that the age of the domain made this a costly, but non-permanent mistake.

With help from their web team, we re-created content relevant to their targeted keywords.

Since the old, aged pages had been deleted; we created 301-pages redirecting them to the new pages. This told Google and other major search engines that the aged pages were still there, just moved.

Doing this re-established the page authority for most of the products, leaving us with only the competitors to deal with.

We found that fixing the aged pages was half the battle. We tackled the other half with money. By contacting well know news sources and putting out press we were able to secure links from major news outlets and traffic sources.

Having both time and money back on our side, we were able to secure the former rankings, driving traffic and sales back to their previous levels.

Going forward, their team now knows to keep an eye on historical content that is well aged to make sure it is contributing to the overall health of the site. Their rankings continue to improve, driving a gap between them and their competitors with less age or budget.

Things to Ponder

1. What short tail keywords are major traffic drivers in your industry?

2. What sites currently get most of the short tail keyword traffic? How old are these sites? How well are they known? Are they websites

that have authority beyond your own?

3. What type of budget would you need to compete on the same level as your competitors for your industry short tail keywords?

4. How broadly do your short tail keywords match your product or service? How many sales could stem from the keyword if it came up in searches? (Remember the "egg" example.)

End of Chapter Challenge

This chapter challenge isn't meant to discourage you, but should give you some perspective. Understanding the challenge is the first step to overcoming it.

Choose a short tail keyword with over 100,000 searches per month using the Ahrefs Keyword Explorer [7].
Keyword _____

Research the top websites ranking for this keyword in Google, Yahoo, and Bing. Below, write below the data you find on each one.

If you are unsure where to find the data, use questions from a Google search to find the data. Example: "How old is this website.com?"

Domain 1 _____

Age of domain _____

Page Authority _____ Domain Authority _____

Domain 2 _____

Age of domain _____

Page Authority _____ Domain Authority _____

Domain 3 _____

Age of domain _____

Page Authority _____ Domain Authority _____

Now do the same analysis for your own domain and compare with each of your answers.

Your domain _____

Age of domain _____

Page Authority _____ Domain Authority _____

What did you find? If your domain is new, most likely the differences are very stark. If you have a domain that is well aged with high traffic, you may be very competitive.

Next, determine what it will take for you to compete with your competitors for the short tail keyword you targeted.

Use Adwords [8] to research the CPC for the short tail keyword you're targeting. Usually you can expect a 5% click-through for a well-optimized campaign. Multiply .70% of the CPC times .05% of the keyword volume to find the budget.

Budget for Advertising _____

Multiply the number of years by $10,000 to find the SEO budget needed to make up the gap between authority and the age of the domain.

Difference in Age Domain Years _____
Based on those numbers you should have a very broad idea of what it will take to be initially competitive for that specific short tail keyword.

There are other factors you can include such as press, guest blogging, offline marketing, and more, that can allow you to reach more of the audience. For our purposes, we will just measure the age and budget of CPC on Adwords to determine the feasibility of ranking for this keyword.

Citations

[1] Raven Tools, What are Short Tail Keywords?, https://raventools.com/marketing-glossary/short-tail-keywords/

[2] Incredible Egg, http://www.incredibleegg.org/egg-nutrition/

[3] SEO Pressor, Short Tail or Long Tail http://seopressor.com/blog/short-tail-or-long-tail-keywords/

[4] Nikhil Ganotra, Ranking for Short Tail Keywords https://www.universalbloggingtips.com/rank-short-tail-keywords/

[5] Flippa, The entrepreneurs marketplace, http://flippa.com

[6] Godaddy Auctions, http://auctions.godaddy.com

[7] ahrefs Keyword Explorer, https://ahrefs.com/keywords-explorer

[8] adwords, Keyword Planner http://adwords.google.com

Online Resources

Online resources for this chapter can be found at:

https://josephstevenson.com/little-book-keyword-research-ch6/

Links to citations, discussions and submission of additional resources by readers are available for each chapter.

To be notified of future books in the Little Book on Digital Marketing Series please email littlebook@josephstevenson.com or visit our website at http://josephstevenson.com/little-book/ and enter your email in the form provided.

07

Long Tail Keywords

The Low Hanging Fruit of
Keyword Research

"Surely it is a magical thing for a handful of words, artfully arranged, to stop time. To conjure a place, a person, a situation, in all its specificity and dimensions. To affect us and alter us, as profoundly as real people and things do."

- Jhumpa Lahiri

Why

My Myopic Vision

Long tail keywords weren't obvious to me at first. I, like many digital marketers, wanted to focus on the six and seven-digit big traffic producing keywords that everyone wanted. Short tail keywords were glamorous, and so for a time, I stayed focused on them.

I knew going after uber-competitive keywords would be difficult, but I had hoped that hours of work would pay off and I would only need one or two of these keywords to hit the digital marketing jackpot. For years, I basically ignored long tail keywords, focusing instead on very short key phrases that took a lot of work to rank in search engines.

I spent a lot of time on keywords that never ranked higher than page two, and it was very discouraging.

It wasn't until I stumbled on long tail keywords that I realized the benefits they offered. I was doing some keyword research through Ahrefs [1] on a Saturday while my kids were napping. I was looking for some short tail keywords that could drive a lot of traffic and leads to a website, without having to put in more than a few months of work.

I was researching the keyword "small business SEO," which had a difficulty score of forty-three. Ouch! On top of that, there were only three hundred fifty monthly searches nationwide for that phrase, which made it very unattractive.

My audience and best clientele are small business owners, so although this keyword seemed to be a very good match, ranking it was going to be near impossible.

Then I noticed a suggested keyword right above the small business SEO keyword. It was "small business SEO packages." For me, the surprising part was the keyword difficulty for this phrase was four. In case you think that's a typo -- I'll confirm that the difficulty was a single digit number four. The search volume was three hundred per month nationwide, which was higher than the original keyword I was researching.

At this point I remembered what Syed Balkhi, chief editor at WPBeginner, shared in his post on long tail keywords; 70% of queries on search engines are long tail keyword searches [2]. I understood this instantly, because right below the long tail keyword were hundreds of related keywords driving between 10 and 30 hits per month.

I felt a little silly that I had focused so heavily on short tail keywords. I almost missed out on the gold mine found in long tail keywords.

Myopic vision is human nearsightedness; when you can clearly see close objects, but farther away objects are blurred. I had focused so much on short tail keywords that long tail keywords were completely out of focus.

Even if you're bad at math, you can understand that one short, super competitive keyword getting three hundred searches per month cannot compete with one hundred less competitive keywords driving seven times the amount of traffic.

Additionally, it's better to spread risk across

multiple keywords instead of having all of your eggs in just one or two high volume keyword baskets. This is generally just good business, but something I hadn't thought about in my early targeting.

Multiple Applications

You might be thinking, "Thanks for the lesson on the habits of search engine users but how does this help me? I'm not focusing on Google!"

Great question! According to Neil Patel in his "7 Brilliant Examples of Brand Driving Long Tail Organic Traffic" [3], Amazon makes 57% of their sales from long tail keywords. If most purchases are coming from long tail keywords that must also add real value beyond SEO -- like ecommerce or product sales.

Amazon has quickly become another large search engine but is completely different from search engines like Google.

Amazon users are already in a buying mindset. They're either researching or looking for good deals on products they want to acquire.

Regular search engines have some product searches as well, but they are mixed with educational, blog, research, news, and a ton of other queries that could be produced by anyone from kindergartener to a grandmother.

I'm not going to spend time talking about the difference between Google and Amazon, but I bring them up to illustrate my point: Long tail keywords dominate large search engine sites regardless of what type of user they service. Understanding this can give you an edge over competitors and others who think like I initially did about long tail keywords.

Although I mention Google and Amazon, there are obviously thousands of sites that can drive traffic based on your keyword research. We haven't even touched on social media, forums, blogs, banner ads, remarketing or PPC.

There are so many online traffic sources that it would be impossible to cover them all.

What I do hope to accomplish is a broad understanding of how long tail keywords can work to benefit your company.

Don't get stuck in the trap of thinking that hundreds of keywords with ten to fifty searches per month won't be as valuable as one keyword that gets five thousand. It's tempting to go after the big kahuna keywords, but it's much sweeter to see immediate and sustainable traffic/sales for keywords that rank more easily.

Long tail keywords are everywhere and important regardless of where you're focusing your digital marketing efforts. Whether you're targeting Google, Amazon, Facebook, Wikipedia, or any other major website, long tail keywords must be researched and chosen before you do anything else.

If you don't take this step first you might as well guess wildly on where to focus your time and hope that it pays off.

How

The Selection Process

Targeting long tail keywords is an addition to targeting short tail keywords. The general idea is to find short tail keywords with low difficulty scores and high volume to produce sufficiently powerful long tail keywords.

Our "small business SEO" key phrase is actually an example of a bad short tail keyword. It's certainly one we wouldn't want to use to target long tail keywords. The difficulty score is almost 50, with less than 1,000 unique searches per month. Most of the long tail keywords that would spinoff from this short tail keyword will have so little volume that the return would be minimal to none.

Proper Targeting and Selection

The proper way to find and target long tail keywords is to first find the appropriate short tail keyword. I will illustrate with an example and step-by-step process.

Using the Ahrefs keyword explorer [1] I found the following data in about 10 minutes. You can use the same process.

Select the Short Tail. First, I entered "SEO" to the keyword tool. The search volume is 134,000 per month and the keyword difficulty is 92. (Definitely a fine candidate for short tail keyword!) Since I have a nice, broad short tail, it's time to go to the next step. If you have trouble, just remember to use a category. For example, if you are a termite expert look for pests or pest control.

Research the Long Tail Keywords. Under "Search suggestions full report," I can sort by KD, which is the second column. If I sort from lowest to highest, I will see a lot of searches with no volume or KD. Usually I will skip to page three or four, but if you have time, look through each page for relevant low-hanging fruit.

Select Based on KD and Volume. By page four I spotted what I'm looking for. The keyword phrase "SEO analyst" has 400 searches per month and a difficulty score of zero.

Based on this data I should be able to rank this keyword fairly easily. My only worry is that the CPC is $10 so it will probably fill up with competitors quickly. Let's find a better one.

The next keyword I see with potential is "SEO writing jobs." It has similar search volume, but the CPC is only $3. Additionally, the KD is zero. This could be a good one, since I'm always looking for good writers, but I still don't think it's quite good enough -- so I'll keep looking.

Finally, on page 12 I find a very nice result. The keyword "SEO for photographers" has 200 searches per month. The KD is nine and the CPC is $10. This is a highly targeted keyword since the majority of people searching are photographers looking for an SEO service. I can create a nice landing page showcasing my skill at ranking photographers, with special fees targeted just to that audience.

Once I rank well I can also consider PPC to own multiple spots in search engines for this keyword.

Don't be Impatient

Take your time paging through possible keywords for just the right ones. Don't get in the high volume mindset, since that is really more of an short tail keyword game. Instead, look for highly targeted keywords with low KD and the lowest CPC you can find. This will allow you to target the keywords that others aren't.

The time you put into ranking your content will pay off in more ways than one. In the last chapter I talked about how the time a page is up can make a bid difference in ranking. As the Internet ages, keywords will only get more difficult to rank for. Searching and targeting easy-to-rank long tail keywords will put time on your side.

Creating a properly ranked page now will be very hard to beat a few years down the road when someone targets your keywords. You'll put time on your side and only those with enough capital and guts will have a chance at taking you on.

Case Study

OSHA Training

A client hired us to help them get better search engine rankings for their OSHA safety training kit. Even though they have been around for more than twenty-five years, they haven't been able to get to page one on search engines for industry-related short tail keywords.

After analyzing current traffic, we found the majority of their visitors were already coming from Google at a rate of about 5,000 unique visitors per month. They were not doing a lot of consistent blogging and their site was running on a shared server with a bad load time.

We decided the best strategy would be to optimize their current website to rank since the age of their domain allowed some pretty old high quality backlinks, making off-site SEO not much of an issue.

We moved their site to WP Engine [4] and upgraded their site to a Wordpress [5] version with Woocommerce [6] running their cart. After optimizing the site for speed we moved to content.

Their rankings told us some of the higher traffic keywords were not driving visitors, and they also didn't show up for many long tail keywords. With that in mind, we decided to adjust their page content to blanket the industry instead of having just a few key phrases.

We adjusted the copy page by page to focus more on OSHA-related forklift safety training. The results were pretty amazing.

After eight months, the site's traffic doubled to 10,000 unique hits per month. We also saw revenue go up by thirteen percent (13%) from the same time the year before. Our analysis showed users interacted with the site the same as they always had except there were just more of them.

The most important sign that the strategy had paid off was that the site was not ranking any higher for the competitive keywords we had identified at the beginning of our engagement. All of the traffic was coming from the long tail keywords we identified and targeted with basic on-page SEO.

Things to Ponder

1. What long tail keywords can you think of without using tools to detect them? Why would people search for these keywords? What would be their intention?

2. What is your reason for targeting these keywords? Be perfectly honest with yourself. Is it money, authority, fame, or something else?

3. Does your intent match the intent of the user? For example, if someone is looking for cheap baseball gloves, is that what you're offering?

4. How difficult will it be to capture audiences from these long tail keywords? How much work will you have to do?

5. What content do you already have that could rank for long tail keywords without a lot of effort?

End of Chapter Challenge

This end of chapter challenge will require you to find a long tail keyword to write about that will drive over 1,000 searches per month. Start by picking a short tail keyword that has a difficulty score under 30. Write it below:

Short tail keyword _____

Difficulty _____ Volume _____

Next add the keyword into the Ahrefs keyword research tool [1] located at https://ahrefs.com/keywords-explorer. Verify that the keyword difficulty score is fewer than 30, and if so, review the keyword ideas listed below the main keyword.

For the purposes of this exercise, pick a

keyword suggestion that has at least three or at least two additional words attached to the short tail keyword. This will allow easier ranking than long tail keywords that just barely make the cut. List the long tail keyword below:

Long tail keyword _____

Difficulty _____ Volume _____

Write a blog, press release, or other public content in web format, targeting the long tail keyword. Set your minimum length to 1,000 words with the long tail keyword as the focus. Don't use the keywords more than 2.5% of the time or 25 times for every 1,000 words.

This exercise is not meant to benefit you other than in terms of education, so feel free to have fun and contribute to someone else's blog or Wikipedia page. Whatever sounds fun and has a low probability of failure based on the above requirements. Publish the content and list the page here.

URL to content: _____

Track your Google rankings over the next five weeks. You're looking for improvement in the rankings for your content.

Week	1	2	3	4	5
Ranking					

If this exercise doesn't produce the expected results, try different keywords or multiple keywords at the same time to get a feel for content creation around long tail keywords. Additional tracking tables are listed below for your convenience:

Long tail keyword _____

Difficulty _____ Volume _____

Week	1	2	3	4	5
Ranking					

Long tail keyword _____

Difficulty _____ Volume _____

Week	1	2	3	4	5
Ranking					

Long tail keyword _____

Difficulty _____ Volume _____

Week	1	2	3	4	5
Ranking					

Long tail keyword _____

Difficulty _____ Volume _____

Week	1	2	3	4	5
Ranking					

Long tail keyword _____

Difficulty _____ Volume _____

Week	1	2	3	4	5
Ranking					

Citations

[1] Ahrefs Keyword Research Tool
https://ahrefs.com/keywords-explorer

[2] Syed Balkhi, How We Increased Our Organic Search Traffic By Using HitTail http://www.wpbeginner.com/wp-tutorials/how-we-increased-our-organic-search-traffic-by-using-hittail/

[3] Neil Patel, 7 Brilliant Examples of Brand Driving Long Tail Organic Traffic http://neilpatel.com/blog/7-brilliant-examples-of-brands-driving-long-tail-organic-traffic/

[4] WP Engine http://wpengine.com

[5] Wordpress http://wordpress.org

[6] Woocommerce http://woocommerce.com

Online Resources

Online resources for this chapter can be found at: https://josephstevenson.com/little-book-keyword-research-ch7/

Links to citations, discussions and submission of additional resources by readers are available for each chapter.

To be notified of future books in the Little Book on Digital Marketing Series please email littlebook@josephstevenson.com or visit our website at http://josephstevenson.com/little-book/ and enter your email in the form provided.

08

Exact Match

For Extremely Targeted Content

"Fast is fine, but accuracy is everything."

- Wyatt Earp

Why

The Possibilities

Exact match keywords are a controversial subject. That's because Google killed them off when many SEO companies targeting them too specifically. Although this changed happened, a lot of companies still target exact match keywords and see good results from their efforts.

So, on one side you have people shouting exact match keywords don't work, while people on the other side are sharing results that defy what should and shouldn't work.

Exact match targeting was much like the early SEO years when you could add a target keyword to your website 50 times in the footer and you would rank for it. Instead of stuffing the page with keywords, many marketers would use a phrase to brand their page and their business in hopes of getting more traffic.

Google, hoping to incentivize companies to create useful content that wasn't targeted to a specific keyword, killed off exact match in their algorithm [1]. You can still utilize exact match keywords for ads as seen in the support area of Adwords [2].

In their documentation Google explained:

Ads may show on searches that match the exact term or are close variations of that exact term. Close variations here may also include a reordering of words if it doesn't change the meaning, and the addition or removal of function words (prepositions, conjunctions, articles, and other words that don't impact the intent of a search).

- Symbol: [keyword]
- Example keyword: [women's hats]
- Example search: hats for women

So exact match isn't necessarily dead, it has just become broadened by topical searches that are closely related.

Pros of Exact Match

Searching for most things online can be a headache if you aren't clear about what you're looking for. If you type in "dog" you will get everything in the world about dogs.

With exact match you can remove doubt from your search. Instead of Google showing suggestions or ads to people who are "close" to what you are searching for, they would only show it to people who actually searched for what you allowed.

This is extremely helpful for specific industries where qualified candidates look for specific search terms in order to find an exact product.

Additionally, it is easier to spend money on ads or SEO to be in front of people who search for "premium dog biscuits for $30" than for a search like "premium biscuits."

Targeting exactly what the user searches for allows you to remove doubt about how aligned your ads or pages are with the user's intent.

Most importantly, having this ability to focus your efforts around a highly-converting set of keywords can improve the ROI of campaigns dramatically [3].

Cons of Exact Match

With every pro there's a con, and the same is true with exact match keywords.

Many marketers caught on to the benefit of only showing for highly profitable keywords. That would immensely drive up the competition for some keywords, while others went unnoticed. This presented a very big problem for Google and other search engines when trying to sort out rankings.

Imaging 90% of websites targeting a few keywords with none targeting keywords that didn't produce a high= search volume. You end up with a bad search experience for users and unsatisfied content creators who feel like they wasted time.

After all, long tail makes up a huge amount of search traffic. Until recently not many people tapped into that. By adjusting the algorithm, Google forced marketers to broaden their keyword base away from exact match.

Besides the increased cost, exact match poses a huge problem for new entrants with no age or authority who seek to enter the Internet.

Ranking number one in ads or SEO for "premium dog biscuits for $30" would be virtually impossible if that was everyone's exact target.

Many short tail keywords that serve as an exact match gold mines are still extremely hard to rank for, but with the changes made by Google it has evened the playing field a little.

What is Really Going on

As of today, josephstevenson.com ranks well for some targeted exact match keywords. If you type in "Las Vegas SEO" we usually rank very close to, if not number one.

The same holds true for many other cities we work in.

When the changes came out, we, like many others, saw a rakings decrease due to our focus only on that exact keyword phrase. With the majority of our clients using that term to find us it was our big money maker at the time.

We decided to fix the issue by changing our content to focus on the SEO industry as a whole. Over a short period, we were able to regain rankings, adding more stable keywords to target.

The same holds true for most industries. You have to target broadly to get your exact match keywords.

If you don't, you may see short-term success, but usually nothing that lasts very long. A solid strategy is to find your exact match keywords and then create your media to focus on all related keywords.

The idea is in averaging. By focusing on a set of keywords that make up your exact match phrase you are sending signals to Google about your main topic. Exact match is a set of keywords in a specific order. By adjusting the order or number of keywords you broaden the target and still maintain the topic.

How

The Selection Process

As mentioned previously, exact match keywords can be long or short tail. The idea isn't in the length or difficulty but instead in the targeting. Exact match is any keyword that you know will sell your product or service.

If you sell horseshoes for a dollar and people search for "horseshoes for a dollar" you are going to want to target that keyword phrase.

In order to get the exact match keyword though you have to broadly target with your main focus pointing at a specific exact match phrase.

Select the Topic. Using our keyword explorer tool [4] we can find the right keywords to target that will give us an exact match. For this example, I searched for "$100 SEO."

The results came up with a big fat zero. No searches per month. No big deal, since I'm not worried about that right now.

Below the result is the "Keyword Ideas" column. In order the following keywords were listed with their volume:

100 dollars SEO	50
100 SEO	40
Top 100 SEO directories	10
SEO100 tips	10
SEO top 100	10

You will hopefully notice a pattern in the suggested keywords. Each one contains a word from our search phrase which contained "100" and "SEO." This is a very important thing to remember.

When finding your most valuable exact match keywords, don't worry about whether someone searches for it. Research what you know will sell and find the closest related keyword(s).

Research the volume and difficulty. By clicking on the keyword ideas report we can see a full list of suggested keywords that contain the words from our phrase.

I can see that the most targeted exact match keyword is "100 dollars SEO." In the past, I would target that keyword alone and forget the rest. With the latest changes from Google I have to broaden my scope a little to be effective.

Like the other chapters we need to check that the KD and volume are in line with our goals or we're wasting our time.

The KD on this one is zero and the volume is 50, which would usually be too low for me.

For educational purposes I will pretend like the traffic is a little higher and choose this as my keyword I want to target.

Create and Promote the Content with Variations. Knowing your exact match keyword allows you to decide how to promote it. Since we are targeting "100 dollar SEO," we need to create content focused on that topic.

Following Google's new rules, our strategy should be to target as many keyword variations as we can in our content and then promote it in the same way.

Keywords might include "100 dollar SEO,", "SEO for 100 dollars," $100 dollar SEO," "one hundred dollar SEO," etc. Beyond close variations like this, you should also plan to use keywords in your content and marketing that aren't as close.

These could include keywords like "SEO top 100," "SEO 100 tips," etc. Having two out of the three keywords match is a good sign; search engines will consider you a close match with wide keyword distribution throughout your website.

This is how sites naturally rank organic rewards; they go to those who are the most natural, or at least appear to be.

Tying it all Together

Keyword rankings for ads and organic search change frequently -- more so than anything else in digital marketing. It seems like every month the search engines are changing rules to make it more difficult to capture clients based on searches.

The difficulties are not just in organic rankings but ad networks, as well. Keeping up with targeting rules can be a major headache for companies trying to market their business online.

With this in mind, the idea of broadly targeting specific keyword phrases to average your rankings for exact match keywords might be a bad idea in a few years. The principle is sound, but with ever-changing search engine rules, the risks that it will become outdated is high.

However, the principal of creating good content that naturally covers a topic containing an exact match keyword should stick around for a while.

In our marketing efforts we have never had issues with a client's or our own website losing market share because we created too much quality content.

It's tempting to think search engines are out to punish website owners, but the truth is they are trying to show the most relevant results. As long as your content deserves to be in front of users, changes to algorithms shouldn't affect your keyword ranking strategy. **Quality and intent** will almost always trump gaming the system when it comes to keyword research and targeting.

Case Study

Embroidery

A long-time client of ours is a Las Vegas based printing and embroidery shop. When we started working for them the main target keyword was embroidery.
The highest volume keyword at the time was the exact match keyword "Las Vegas Embroidery."

At the time, we were able to build our entire strategy based on ranking for this one keyword. All of our content and marketing was directed at this exact match keyword in hopes of driving the most qualified leads to the business.

After about six months, they finally hit the number one Google ranking, which skyrocketed sales. The value of having every exact match search for embroidery show them as number one was phenomenal.

After a couple of years, we noticed rankings slipping despite a very clean marketing plan and website. This was right around one of the keyword updates on Google.

After research, we found that they were too targeted at the one exact match phrase. They had grown their business to offer business cards, banners, screen printing and more, but their main target had always been embroidery.

To increase their rankings back to where they were, we decided to broaden their target to keywords around embroidery that weren't an exact match.

We also targeted the other services they offered with the term "Las Vegas" inserted. By having the site branded and marketed as "Las Vegas" with content talking about embroidery, printing, t-shirt printing, etc. it broadened the scope and restored the initial rankings.

Although it took six months originally to rank the site for their main exact match keyword, broadening the scope and restoring the rankings only took about two months.

This goes back to offering value in your content that will surpass updates and rankings changes.

Since we used clean marketing methods, when Google did their update, they dropped our rankings. It wasn't a drop due to a penalty.
Instead we were less relevant after the update, which only required us to make changes to the site, not retract what we had already done.

Today they still enjoy high rankings due to a long-term strategy and broad base of keywords that focus on exact match using an average of all targeted keywords.

Things to Ponder

1. What exact match keyword(s) would drive the most targeted traffic to your brand?

2. Of the exact match keywords, how much volume and competition is there? What is the KD for the keywords?

3. What related keywords support the exact match keywords selected? Are the related keywords purchased keywords, or keywords people use when buying?

4. Of the related keywords how targeted are they to your brand? How many of the keywords contain the same phrases as the exact match keyword?

End of Chapter Challenge

Since the main point of exact match keywords is to drive the most targeted visitors to your media, this end of chapter challenge will focus on that main goal.

Below, put the most targeted exact match keyword for your business. Don't worry about whether there is any volume for the keyword, only make sure it is a keyword that if searched would almost guarantee a conversion of the searcher to your product or service:

Exact match keyword _____

Next using the Ahrefs Keyword Planner [4] find the related keywords that contain the same words as your exact match keyword. Put the three most related keywords below with their volume and KD.

Related Keyword 1 _____
Keyword Difficulty _____Volume _____

Related Keyword 2 _____
Keyword Difficulty _____Volume _____

Related Keyword 3 _____
Keyword Difficulty _____Volume _____

These three keyword phrases should be the focus in your marketing efforts to naturally target your exact match keyword.

You should still target your exact match keyword, but a good rule of thumb is 80/20. Target 80% of your marketing to the keywords that are related to your exact match keyword, and 20% to the exact match keyword directly.

Finally, do some searches in Google with your related keywords to see what websites already rank for them.

Research their pages and content to see how many are using the exact phrase, and how many are using broad terms that contain parts of the phrase.

Look through the title and site meta tags. You'll find them below the blue link and the text description in the search results. See how many of the results contain the phrase exactly and how many contain only portions of the phrase.

Citations

[1] Google Adwords Killed "Exact Match", Kissmetrics, https://blog.kissmetrics.com/adwords-killed-exact-match/

[2] About keyword matching options, Google, https://support.google.com/adwords/answer/2497836?hl=en

[3] Anvil, Improve Adwords ROI with search terms,
http://www.anvilmediainc.com/2014/01/16/improving-adwords-roi-with-search-terms-report/

[4] Ahrefs Keyword Explorer,
https://ahrefs.com/keywords-explorer

Online Resources

Online resources for this chapter can be found at:

https://josephstevenson.com/little-book-keyword-research-ch8/

Links to citations, discussions and submission of additional resources by readers are available for each chapter.

To be notified of future books in the Little Book on Digital Marketing Series please email littlebook@josephstevenson.com or visit our website at http://josephstevenson.com/little-book/ and enter your email in the form provided.

09

Broad and Phrase Match

More Traffic Potential

"I didn't feel like a giant. I felt very, very small."

- Neil Armstrong

Why

How Broad and Phrase Match Work

In general, the broader the keyword matching option, the more traffic potential it has. Conversely, the narrower the keyword matching option, the more relevant it will be to someone's search.

Understanding these differences can help you choose the right options and improve your ROI. Don't take my word for it; here is the exact text from the manage section of Adwords help [1]:

> Broad and phrase match keywords are different from each other and can affect how your advertising is run through Adwords and other networks who use a similar strategy.

Beyond paid ads, these two keyword types are also applicable in social and organic marketing; although this isn't broadly talked about.

Both broad and phrase match are determined similarly to our example in the last chapter -- with just a few variations. To make understanding them easier, I will add Google's explanation and my own interpretation for each one.

Broad Match

From Google:

When you use broad match, your ads automatically run on relevant keyword variations, even if those terms aren't on your keyword lists. This will help you attract more website visitors, spend less time building keyword lists, and focus your spending on keywords that work.

Broad match is the default match type that all your keywords are assigned to, unless you specify another match type (exact match, phrase match, or negative match).

Google AdWords automatically runs ads with relevant keyword variations, including synonyms, singular and plural forms, possible misspellings, stemming's (such as *floor* and *flooring*), related searches, and other relevant variations. To help deliver relevant matches, this match type may also take the customer's recent search activities into account.

An example would be the keyword "low-carb diet plan". The broad match keywords you might also show up for are:

- Carb-free foods
- Low-carb diets
- Low calorie recipes
- Mediterranean diet plans
- Low-carbohydrate dietary program

Broad match is helpful for targeting groups of individuals interested in the general subject. So, low-carbs, dieting, low calories, etc.

The benefits of marketing this way are endless, especially for businesses that are looking to blanket an entire industry.

Facebook and other social platforms use a similar approach by allowing advertisers to show ads to users based on their general interests. For example, I'm able to target users who are a certain age and demographic through keyword research. It is still a broad match, since they may be interested in anything related to the subject, but it is helpful if I need a lot of eyes on my media.

Phrase Match

More from Google:

With phrase match, your ad can appear when people search for your exact phrase, even if they include one or more words before or after it. We'll also show your ad when someone searches for a close variant of your phrase match keyword. Close variants include misspellings, singular and plural forms, acronyms, stemmings (such as *floor* and *flooring*), abbreviations, and accents. Word order is important with phrase match, meaning that your ad won't appear if someone enters an additional word in the middle of your keyword.

Phrase match is more flexible than exact match, but is more targeted than the default broad match option. With phrase match, you can reach more customers, while still showing your ads to customers who are most likely searching for your product or service.

The last paragraph from Google is worth its weight in gold and worth repeating:

Phrase match is more flexible than exact match (remember that exact match means it needs to be exactly what is typed in), but is more targeted than the default broad match option (broad match gets the whole industry but not so targeted). With phrase match, you can reach more customers, while still showing your ads to customers who are most likely searching for your product or service.

What is Your Choice?

There is no keyword option perfect for everyone. Exact, broad, or phrase keywords work differently for everyone.

Understanding the purpose of each can help you determine the keyword to match your marketing plan.

In the following paragraphs, I'll define the purpose for each type of keyword. Which one matches what you're trying to accomplish?

Exact Match: As the name implies it is a marketing strategy to show your media to searchers with the exact keyword you specify. It's very targeted and narrow.

Broad Match: Blankets entire keyword topics and industries. Usually used by companies looking for massive exposure to a large audience.

Phrase Match: A mix between the other two, it combines exact match with broad to deliver results that are less defined than exact, but with very close keyword variations.

Regardless of your marketing sources, each keyword type should be considered during the planning stages.

SEO, Adwords, Facebook, and any other traffic source utilize each keyword type in one form or another.

Failure to properly pick the type of keyword most applicable to your business could result in a very bad ROI for your company.

This is not to be meant as a warning, but instead an understanding, so you can properly determine, and then target the right kind of keyword for your business.

How

Using Broad and Phrase Match

Since broad and phrase match keywords are different, we will discuss each in detail along with how to properly target and utilize them.

Broad Match

Knowing that broad is going to cover a very large area with interests generally related, we need to know where our most likely audience is.

I am an SEO consultant for large SEO firms and marketing departments who need digital marketing expertise.

I have found that my target audience spends time in places like Search Engine Land [2], MOZ Blog [3], SEO Chat Forums [4], and Ahrefs [5].

Each of these options has different opportunities for me to reach out to their users.

Search Engine Land has multiple advertising options including a dedicated email to subscribers and ads throughout the site.

MOZ allows user submitted content, so I am able to create engaging content related to SEO for free exposure. The only thing I need to invest is time.

SEO chat forums allow me to post my opinion on threads and share advice to newbies and seasoned SEO consultants alike.

Ahrefs has a blog and support area that I can engage in to share insights into what works for me.

Although all of these sites are related to what I do, they may not be the best place for me to advertise unless I am going after a broad match.

Remember that all of these sites might have different visitors using them. Users looking to hire an SEO, users who are actual SEO specialists, or users who are students looking into SEO as a career. There may be the occasional misspelling of a South Korean city, as well, that misleads some users, which may disrupt the process.

If I have a product or service that appeals to the majority of the people on these sites, then it's probably a great idea to target them.

If, however, I am targeting something more specific, it's probably not the best place to be putting time and resources.

Only you can decide the right keyword for your business. Understanding how and where to look for broad match keywords can help determine if they are right for you.

Phrase Match

Phrase match keywords are harder to target,

but usually more profitable for companies with defined audiences and products/services.

The easiest way to target phrase match keywords is through SEO and ad networks like Adwords.

SEO

You can create website pages targeting the general phrase or topic you're looking to market by using SEO. Google's algorithm is now able to display your website results based on the phrase you're targeting.

Google has started recommending that site owners create content around topics that are naturally written versus being written for the exact match keyword.

Pages should now read more like:

American Beauty Salon. A Las Vegas based hair salon serving the valley for over 20 years!

Instead of how they used to read to target

exact match keywords:

Las Vegas Hair Salon American Beauty is a Las Vegas Hair Salon based in the Las Vegas Valley. We are a 20-year-old Las Vegas Hair Salon.

Just writing that makes me feel sick in my stomach, but unfortunately this has been the go-to way of ranking "naturally" for years. Stay away from it and for your own sanity keep your content focused on the phrase, not the exact match.

Ad Networks

This is the easiest option for targeting phrase match keywords. For example, Adwords has a setting to designate phrase match keywords as options for your ads.

Other networks like Facebook, Bing, and display ads allow targeting based on interests and keywords.

YouTube is another example that piggybacks on Adwords PPC, allowing targeting based on interests and keyword searches.

My recommendation to all businesses is to work through an ad network before spending time on other options like SEO or content marketing.

Ad networks are able to deliver immediate results versus the longer-term strategy that comes with SEO or content marketing.

Testing your muse through an ad network will save time and resources for products that don't perform well regardless of the keyword type.

Case Study

Hospice Care

One of our SEO clients provides hospice services in Las Vegas, Henderson and Pahrump, Nevada.

When we began working together we noticed that they had decent organic rankings for their business name, but they also had potential to naturally rank for hospice-related keywords.

Due to the sensitive nature of their work we wanted to be as careful as we could to promote their services in a kind and compassionate way.

We found that having thoughtful content around hospice care and end-of-life circumstances allowed those searching for it to find information that was helpful and sensitive.

Using phrase match keywords as our strategy, we were able to target specific language that searchers were looking.

Searches like, "How much does hospice cost?" and "When should I put my loved one in a hospice?" were phrases we worked on to put this organization in front of searchers.

The results have been spectacular, and the individuals who end up using hospice services have appreciated the kind way they were able to find and receive care.

Although we were a little torn between using broad or phrase match keywords in our strategy, we decided phrase would be better for targeted those in need versus those researching for school or business.

We weren't opposed to others finding the site, but we definitely didn't want to be commercially driven and risk hurting those who needed this care for themselves or a loved one.

Things to Ponder

1. What broad or phrase match keyword(s) would drive the most targeted traffic to your brand?

2. How large is the audience if you were to target only broad match keywords?

3. How large is the audience if you were to target phrase match only?

4. How targeted are the broad match keywords to your product or service? How targeted are the phrase match keywords? Would either be a good fit for your business?

End of Chapter Challenge

This end of chapter challenge will pit keywords against each other. The idea is to determine which would work better.

Both may not be a good fit but this should get you in the right mindset for making these decisions.

Write your audience below. This could be students looking for schools, or moms looking for two-year-old jumpsuits. Whatever it is, try to be as specific as you can.

Audience _____

Next, using Google [6], search for broad keywords that fit your industry. For instance, if you choose students looking for schools it might be a keyword like "best universities" or "best schools on the west coast."

Write down the top three results in Google

and what the pages were intended to have
the user do:

Result _____
Intent _____

Result _____
Intent _____

Result _____
Intent _____

These results should be your broad match
keyword competition. You should be able to
see quickly if the results are too broad or if
the users finding those pages would also be
interested in what you have.

If you want to compete through SEO, take
note of any advertising available on those
pages or how competitive the domains are.

Do the same for phrase match keywords by
picking an exact match keyword, and then
researching through Ahrefs [7] any related
keywords that would make up your phrase
match keywords.

Once you have found keywords that would fall under phrase match do the same exercise with Google to see top results.

Result _____

Intent _____

Result _____

Intent _____

Result _____

Intent _____

Compare each result to determine which audience would be most likely to purchase from you.

Assuming both are good audiences, plan on a five percent (5%) traffic conversion for each one. Calculate the total number of visitors using Ahrefs keyword explorer [8] and multiply by .05.

Depending the cost to target keywords in each area, you should be able to determine which keyword type is right for your business.

Citations

[1] Google Adwords help, https://support.google.com/adwords/answer/2497836?hl=en

[2] Search Engine Land, http://searchengineland.com/

[3] The MOZ Blog, https://moz.com/blog

[4] SEO Chat Forums, http://forums.seochat.com/

[5] Ahrefs, http://ahrefs.com/

[6] Google Search, http://google.com/

[7] Ahrefs Keyword Explorer, https://ahrefs.com/keywords-explorer/

Online Resources

Online resources for this chapter can be found at:

https://josephstevenson.com/little-book-keyword-research-ch9/

Links to citations, discussions and submission of additional resources by readers are available for each chapter.

To be notified of future books in the Little Book on Digital Marketing Series please email littlebook@josephstevenson.com or visit our website at http://josephstevenson.com/little-book/ and enter your email in the form provided.

10

Negative Keywords

It's Important to Know
What you Don't Want

"It's only by saying "no" that you can concentrate on the things that are really important."

- Steve Jobs

Why

What they are

In keyword research and marketing there are times when you need to say, "No" to accepting irrelevant results and keywords.

Keywords that contain the words "free" or

"cheap" are not very favorable for paid products. Additionally, words like "simple" and "easy" shouldn't be used when discussing certain subjects.

In advertising and SEO, there are keywords that could actually produce a negative result for a user. These keywords should be identified and removed from your strategy.

This is a completely normal process and required if you are looking to properly optimize your campaign to target only the most relevant keywords.

Why they Need to be Removed not Just Ignored

Ignoring irrelevant keywords can actually be harmful for a brand. We have had a lot of clients come to us with horror stories of reviews left by people who weren't clients but were offended by keyword targeting mishaps.

What the users were expecting based on their keyword research was not what they found when they clicked on the landing page of our client's site.

Although most people don't easily get offended, there are others who feel it is their duty to troll the Internet and tear down brands either for fun or as a weird vendetta against irrelevant content.

To avoid these self-proclaimed moderators, it is a good idea to identify any negative keywords and remove them from your campaign.

Removing negative keywords is easy with ad networks like Adwords [1], but is extremely difficult for organic results.

Organic results are populated based on how a crawler interacts with your website. If the crawler categorizes you too broadly, you may show up for keywords you don't want. This can create an especially difficult problem for regulated industries.

Occasionally sites will show up for products or services that have nothing to do with what they offer [2] causing user confusion and lost sales for the brand.

The Solution is in the Content

In the next section, we'll discuss the process for removing negative keywords from your campaigns.

Identifying and removing negative keywords from ad campaigna is relatively simple. Identifying and labeling negative keywords in organic campaigns will be difficult, but necessary. Let's dig in.

How
Defining and Removing
Negative Keywords

To start, we'll talk about the easy way to remove negative keywords from ad platforms.

Most ad platforms, like Adwords [1], have the ability to identify and select negative keywords.

Identifying Negative Keywords

For both ad networks and organic traffic, it's important to identify all the keywords you're receiving traffic from. Then you can figure out the negative keywords.

Ad Networks. The only way to identify negative keywords for ad networks is to let your ads run for a period of time and then test the data. The old adage that it takes money to make money is especially true in the pay per click world.

By running campaigns for a couple of weeks you will be able to gather keyword data and their impressions. Once you have enough impressions and clicks, you'll be able to see which specific keywords are costing you the most, and how relevant they are.

Ad networks like Amazon's Advertising Platform [3] will correlate pay per click directly to your product purchase. This makes it very easy to track ROI per keyword for each ad.

The keywords that are irrelevant and not producing any sales can be removed and better keywords added.

Organic Campaigns. In organic campaigns you don't pay for keyword placement, so you need to rely on other data to determine which negative keywords are affecting your rankings.

You can use a tool like SEM Rush [4] to track new organic keywords in a website campaign. Although their reporting is not free, the data is extremely useful in seeing what you naturally rank for.

By watching the notifications for new rankings, you'll see how relevant or irrelevant your keywords are. This allows you to identify and work on the removal of undesirable keywords.

Removing Negative Keywords

As mentioned previously, it is much easier to remove negative keywords from ad campaigns than organic campaigns.

Ad Networks. With ad networks you can set your campaign to target only specific phrases, broad, or exact match keywords.

As impressions increase for the keywords in your campaign, you can select the ones that are unhelpful and identify them as negative keywords.

Ad networks like Adwords will allow you to list negative keywords so they won't show up on your ads. This is extremely helpful in drilling down campaigns to the most profitable keywords.

Organic Campaigns. To remove keywords that are selected as negative from organic campaigns you have to strip them from your content.

Search engines only know what content is being crawled, so including any negative keywords in your media can adversely affect your site and cause negative rankings.

We have found that many of our clients show for keywords they don't want anything to do with, simply because of a blog post or other seemingly unrelated content that linked to their site.

Sites even have to be careful not to create content about a subject they dislike, in case they rank for that topic and become guilty by association. Usually this is not a major problem, but definitely something that needs to be considered.

With little effort, we can use tools like Ahrefs [5] or Semrush [4], to see what organic keywords are indexed for our site.

Look under the organic keywords section of Ahrefs for naturally ranked keywords. Reviewing these keywords can help you identify which keywords should be considered negative.

Under the URL column on Ahrefs, you can find which pages are ranking for the negative keyword. This helps to narrow larger sites down to any offending pages that need content re-written or other media removed.

Once the pages ranking for negative keywords are identified, you can then adjust

the content to remove the keywords you
don't want.

Tying things Together

Negative keywords are most often used in
PPC campaigns due to the cost per click.

Most organic traffic is appreciated or ignored
by companies looking for rankings. The idea
that any traffic is good traffic has become the
norm.

The reality is that not all traffic is good;
unrelated keywords that a site does not want
to rank for should be removed.

Having a clean media setup will pay off for a
company in the long run.

Highly focused campaigns without negative
keywords tend to perform better and avoid
trolls, reviews, etc., that could damage them
from the unfulfilled promises associated with
negative keywords.

Even if you feel like organic negative
keywords are the fault of the search engine,

you shouldn't ignore them completely.

Eventually a site that has negative keywords will have a hard time ranking for the keywords you are actually targeting. Much like combating spam and bad reviews from malicious competitors or clients, negative keywords have to be moderated and removed for a healthy campaign.

Case Study

Final Grade Calculator

I mentioned my experience with the final grade calculator blog post we used to test keyword difficulty and traffic.

The story doesn't end with us simply removing the blog post.

After we ranked on the first page for the keyword phrase "final grade calculator" we noticed that our organic rankings for SEO-related items dropping.

Spending a lot of time analyzing everything, from our page code to our backlinks, we finally realized that our test blog was confusing Google.

We had targeted our domain at SEO-related items but had also gotten a lot of buzz about our final grade calculator.

The result ended up sharing ranking between education-related keywords and SEO-related keywords.

The term "final grade calculator" had actually hurt rankings in other areas because it was unrelated to our site content.

At the time, we were testing KD, so it was a mistake that we're still trying to rectify.

The proper way to test would have been to set up a new domain centered on that topic; and then create the blogs.

We were tracking our main site's domain authority and wanted to see how it would handle the keyword we posted there.

After removing the blog post and any links throughout our site, we then had to go through the Internet and work to take down any organic posts linking to our old content, now a 404 page.

The lesson with this case study is to be careful that the content you put on your site is relevant and deserves to be there. Otherwise, it might take years to remove it from everywhere Google finds it on the Internet.

Things to Ponder

1. What negative keywords could adversely affect your brand or media?

2. How ingrained are these keywords to your media? Are they easy to remove?

3. Why are these negative keywords in your media? Was it error on the creator's part, desire by the users, etc.?

4. Of the negative keywords, are any close to what you are targeting? If any are close, does it make sense to repurpose the content to capture that traffic?

5. What negative keywords could pop up later, due to content you have on your site that has not yet been indexed?

End of Chapter Challenge

This end of chapter challenge will focus on locating any negative keywords in your media.

Sometimes this can be a difficult task if you don't know what you're looking for. Some believe that all traffic is good traffic.

If this is your opinion just assume for this activity that you might be wrong. ☺

Write down what your target is. You can also write down what product or service you're selling. The idea is to identify in writing what it is you make your money from.

Target _____

Next, list the keywords that would best describe your target. These should be as close to exact match or phrase match keywords as you can manage.

Keyword 1 _____

Keyword 2 _____

Keyword 3 _____

Next using the Ahrefs overview report, look through the organic keyword list for your domain. Sort by traffic, and write down the top three results. Then, sort by traffic again to see the bottom three results. Write them below:

Top 1 _____

Top 2 _____

Top 3 _____

Bottom 1 _____

Bottom 2 _____

Of the keywords, how many match your target? How many are negative keywords, if any? Continue to look through the list for any possible negative keywords.

Citations

[1] Adwords, http://google.com/adwords/

[2] MOZ, Negative Keywords for SEO, https://moz.com/community/q/negative-keywords-for-seo

[3] Amazon Ad Network, https://advertising.amazon.com/ad-specs/en/aap

[4] SEM Rush, http://semrush.com/

[5] Ahrefs, On-Page Test, http://ahrefs.com/

Online Resources

Online resources for this chapter can be found at:

https://josephstevenson.com/little-book-keyword-research-ch10/

Links to citations, discussions and submission of additional resources by readers are available for each chapter.

To be notified of future books in the Little Book on Digital Marketing Series please email littlebook@josephstevenson.com or visit our website at http://josephstevenson.com/little-book/ and enter your email in the form provided.

11

Resources

My Keyword Research Tools

Throughout this book I have referenced a lot of the same tools I use. I wanted to create a comprehensive resource of tools with instructions on the best ways to use them.

I am not endorsing or getting paid to promote any of these tools, so please take that into account for your own research.

I will be putting a page on my website with some of the resources you found in this book. Please visit:

https://josephstevenson.com/little-book-keyword-research-resources/

If you have any resources for keyword research, please feel free to add them in the comments section of that page.

To be notified of future books in the Little Book on Digital Marketing Series, please email littlebook@josephstevenson.com or visit our website at http://josephstevenson.com/little-book/ and enter your email in the form provided.

Adwords. I use the Adwords keyword planner for PPC advertising and keyword research. It's difficult to get accurate volume numbers, but the cost per click gives valuable insight on the competition. Located at adwords.google.com.

Ahrefs. I use Ahrefs for keyword research and domain health. This tool gives great insight into competitor analysis and keyword difficulty. I spend a lot of time talking about Ahrefs throughout the book; not because they pay me, but because I utilize them heavily in my campaigns. Located at ahrefs.com.

MOZ. Moz is a competitor of Ahrefs but offers a more user-friendly dashboard. They have a lot of analysis tools that will give improvement insights to users. Their keyword planner is also very helpful. Located at moz.com.

Raven Tools. This is a nice reporting tool if you have an SEO agency that sends reports to clients. Their pricing is fair and displays data from Google apps. Located at raventools.com.

SEM Rush. This is another reporting software platform that has very accurate keyword ranking data. They also have really nice tools for keyword analysis and suggestions for improvement. Located at semrush.com.

Google Webmasters. This is a free website analyzer from Google. I especially like their keyword area that shows organic keyword placement and volume of impressions over time. Located at google.com/webmasters.

SE Ranking. I use SE Ranking for their keyword-ranking tool. It is one of the most accurate in the industry and extremely affordable. Located at seranking.com.

Spyfu. This is a great competitor analysis tool that you can use to see what your competitors are doing around keyword targeting. Located at spyfu.com.

Serps. Serps is a free tool that allows you to search for high-value keywords. This is useful for KD and volume analysis. Located at serps.com.

Google Trends. I use Google Trends to see keyword popularity over time. If you're worried about whether a keyword is evergreen, you can just look at the history on Google Trends. Located at google.com/trends.

Majestic SEO. Another research tool that I haven't used a lot, but it definitely deserves a mention. It has many of the same abilities as the other tools I've mentioned. Located at majesticseo.com.

Bing Webmaster Tools. The same as Google, but created for the Bing Search Engine. There isn't one of these sites for Yahoo that I know of, but I believe they generally follow the same strategy. Located at bing.com/webmasters.

Authority Labs. This is a keyword-tracking tool offering live report pages, which is nice if you have clients you need to give real-time access to. Located at authoritylabs.com.

Keyword Revealer. An awesome research tool to show what possible profits are in each keyword. This is one of my favorites for finding long tail keywords. Located at keywordrevealer.com.

Google's Keyword Tool for Adwords. This is a solid online guide from Google. It's helpful for brushing up on some of the basics -- and

not so basics. Located at
support.google.com/adwords.

Keyword Tool. This is one I haven't used a
lot, but it autocompletes keywords that you
type into Google, which will help you with
long tail keyword research. Located at
keywordtool.io.

If I've missed any don't forget to add them at
https://josephstevenson.com/little-book-
keyword-research-resources/.

12

Conclusion

Good Things to Come

By writing this book I hope it can be a roadmap for keyword research. Some of you reading this may be just learning digital marketing, while others may be seasoned, experienced marketers.

No matter where you are in your education, I hope you were able to find something useful from my experiences and stories.

If there are any faults in this book they are purely accidental. I hope the entire book won't be judged based on one or two items that change or become outdated with time.

As I mentioned, I have pages online dedicated to each chapter of the book. My hope is that those reading this book can feel a sense of ownership and share their experiences through comments on the pages.

Feel free to comment and share your opinions on the page related to your experiences when completing the exercises. I will publish all opinions as long as they are not trolling or harassing in nature.

This is the first in a series; I hope to cover digital marketing topics in short book format for every major topic.

If you would like to be notified of new books as they come out, please email littlebook@josephstevenson.com or go to josephstevenson.com and sign up for the mailing list.

Thank you so much for reading and I wish you the best of luck in your keyword research.

About the Author

Joseph Stevenson is an SEO Consultant, Author and Public Speaker. He has over 17 years of experience in digital marketing and is the CEO of Joseph Stevenson SEO, a Nevada based firm.

Made in the USA
Middletown, DE
17 August 2017